Pistachio O
Cookb

100 Recipes for Exploring the Versatility of this
Mighty Nut

Robert Lee

TABLE OF CONTENTS

INTRODUCTION

This cookbook is a celebration of the versatile and flavorful pistachio nut. With 100 mouth-watering recipes featuring pistachios as the star ingredient, you'll discover new and exciting ways to incorporate this nut into your sweet and savory dishes. From creamy pistachio ice cream to hearty pistachio-crusted chicken, there's a recipe for every occasion. Each recipe is accompanied by a beautiful colored image to showcase the delicious results. Whether you're a pistachio lover or just looking for creative ways to add more nuts to your diet, this cookbook is a must-have.

BREAKFAST

1. Pistachio Iced Tea

Makes: 2

INGREDIENTS:
- 2 sachets of Black Tea Assam Tea
- 2 cups Hot water
- 1 teaspoon Rose preserve
- 2 teaspoons Pistachios blanched and slivered
- 2 cloves
- 1/2-inch Cinnamon
- 1 Cardamom
- 1 teaspoon sugar optional
- 1 pinch of Saffron Strands
- 6 Ice Cubes

INSTRUCTIONS
a) Freeze the serving glasses for 10 minutes.
b) Tie the whole spices and the tea in a muslin cloth.
c) Bring the water to a rolling boil. Add the muslin cloth to the boiling water.
d) Let the tea bags and the spice bag steep for 5 minutes.
e) Strain into a bowl. Add the rose preserve and extra sugar.
f) Mix in half the pistachios and stir well.
g) Pour into the frozen glasses.
h) Tip in a few more cubes if required. Top with the remaining pistachios and saffron.
i) Serve chilled immediately.

2. Pistachio biscotti

Makes: 32 servings

INGREDIENTS:
- 2 Eggs
- 1 teaspoon Almond extract
- 1 teaspoon Vanilla extract
- ½ cup Sugar
- 1¾ cup Cake flour
- 1 teaspoon Baking powder
- ¼ teaspoon Salt
- ⅔ cup Shelled pistachio nuts
- 3 ounces Semisweet chocolate, melted

INSTRUCTIONS
a) Heat oven to 350'F. In a medium bowl, beat eggs with an electric mixer on high speed until fluffy. Gradually beat in almond extract, vanilla and sugar until mixture is thick and lemon-colored, scraping down sides of bowl frequently with a rubber spatula.

b) Mix cake flour with baking powder and salt. With a wire whisk, fold into egg mixture until just thoroughly combined. Fold in pistachios.

c) Grease a 10x14" strip down center of two cookie sheets. Spoon half of pistachio mixture down center of each cookie sheet to make a 3x10" log. Bake 30 minutes. Remove from oven; leave oven on.

d) Let logs cool on sheets 5 minutes, or until cool enough to handle.

e) With a serrated knife, cut each log diagonally into 16 slices. Place slices, flat sides down, on cookie sheet and return to oven. Bake 5 minutes. Turn slices over and bake 5-7 minutes, or until golden on both sides. Remove to racks and let stand until cool enough to handle. Spread melted chocolate over one end of biscotti and let cool completely. Store in a tightly covered container. Makes: 32 cookies.

3. Pistachio nut tea bread

Makes: 1 serving

INGREDIENTS:
- 1 Stick butter
- 1 cup Sugar
- 2 Eggs
- 3 cups Orange juice
- Grated peel of 2 oranges
- 12 cups Self-rising flour
- 2 cups Fresh or reconstituted powdered buttermilk
- 1 cup Whole pistachios

INSTRUCTIONS
a) Preheat the oven to 350 degrees F. Grease and flour a 9 x 5 x 3-inch loaf pan. In a large mixing bowl, beat the butter and sugar until well blended.

b) Beat in the eggs, orange juice, and peel until light. Add the flour, alternating with the buttermilk. Fold in the pistachios.

c) Pour into the prepared pan and bake until a skewer inserted into the center comes out clean, about 1 hour.

4. Pistachio and avocado smoothie

Makes: 2 servings

INGREDIENTS:

- 1³/₄oz pistachios
- 1 small avocado, stoned, peeled, and quartered
- 1 teaspoons hemp seed oil
- 2 teaspoons linseed oil
- juice of ½ lemon
- fresh juice of 6 celery stems
- freshly ground black pepper to taste pinch of salt
- 3–4 fresh basil leaves
- a little mineral water

INSTRUCTIONS

a) Put all the ingredients except the mineral water into a blender or food processor and blend until smooth. Add enough mineral water to ensure the smoothie is of a pourable consistency.

b) Serve in glasses, with a sprinkle of finely chopped pistachios on top of each.

5. Pistachio Pancakes With Pistachio Butter

Makes: 4

INGREDIENTS:
- 1 cup all-purpose flour
- 1/3 cup finely ground pistachios
- 2 tablespoons sugar
- 1 teaspoon baking powder
- 1 teaspoon baking soda
- 1/4 teaspoon salt
- 2 large eggs, lightly beaten
- 1 1/4 cups milk
- 1 teaspoon vanilla extract
- 2 tablespoons unsalted butter, melted

PISTACHIO BUTTER
- 3 tablespoons finely ground pistachios
- 6 tablespoons unsalted butter

VANILLA BROWN BUTTER SYRUP
- 2 tablespoons unsalted butter
- 1/2 teaspoon vanilla bean paste
- 1/3 cup maple syrup

INSTRUCTIONS

a) In a large bowl, combine the flour, pistachios, sugar, baking powder, soda and salt. Whisk together until combined. In a smaller bowl, whisk together the eggs, milk, vanilla extract and butter. Add the wet **INGREDIENTS:** to the dry, mixing until smooth and combined.

b) Heat a large skillet or electric griddle over medium heat. Add a bit of butter if desired, then pour 1/4 cup of batter on the hot skillet and repeat, leaving an inch between pancakes. Cook until the pancakes bubble on the top and edges, about 2 minutes. Flip and cook for another minute or two until golden and set. Top the pancakes with the pistachio butter and syrup.

PISTACHIO BUTTER

c) Whisk together the butter and pistachios until combined. You can use it just like this or place it in the fridge to harden a bit. If so, you can wrap it tightly in plastic wrap and store it until needed.

VANILLA BROWN BUTTER SYRUP

d) Heat the butter over medium heat in a saucepan, whisking constantly. Cook until it bubbles and the brown bits appear on the bottom, about 4 to 5 minutes, then quickly stir in the vanilla bean paste and remove it from the heat. While warm, stir it into the maple syrup and serve immediately.

6. Pear Chia Pistachio Breakfast Parfait Jars

Makes: 2

INGREDIENTS:
PEAR CHIA PUDDING:
- ¼ cup pear puree
- ⅓ cup unsweetened vanilla or plain almond milk
- 3 tablespoons chia seeds
- Pear Avocado Pudding:
- 1 ripe avocado
- 1-2 teaspoons honey or coconut nectar, depending on preferred sweetness
- 2 tablespoons pear puree

REMAINING LAYERS & GARNISHES:
- ½ cup of your favourite granola
- ½ cup plain coconut yogurt or vanilla Greek yogurt
- ¼ cup chopped fresh pear
- 2 tablespoons chopped pistachios
- 2 teaspoons honey or coconut nectar

INSTRUCTIONS
a) Begin by preparing the Pear Chia Pudding by adding all of the ingredients to a bowl, mixing until well combined, then let sit in the fridge for 15-20 minutes to thicken.
b) Next, prepare the Avocado Pear Pudding by adding all of the ingredients to a small food processor or baby bullet and pulse until the mixture is smooth. Test the taste and add more honey/coconut nectar if you prefer the avocado pudding to be on the sweeter side.
c) Once the chia pudding has thickened, give it another stir and you are ready to layer all the ingredients.
d) Using two 8 ounce jars, divide the granola, yogurt, chia pudding, and avocado pudding, layering these in any arrangement you prefer between the two jars.

e) Finish by topping each jar with 2 tablespoons of chopped fresh pear and 1 tablespoon of chopped pistachios, then drizzle each jar with 1 teaspoon of honey or coconut nectar.

7. Pistachio Scones

Makes: 8 scones

INGREDIENTS:
- 1 1/2 cups flour
- 1/4 cups sugar
- 1/4 tsp salt
- 1 1/2 tsp baking powder
- 1 tsp lemon zest
- 4 Tbsp butter
- 1/3 cups chopped, shelled pistachios
- 1 egg, lightly beaten
- 2 Tbsp milk

INSTRUCTIONS:
a) Preheat oven to 425F.
b) In a large bowl, mix together flour, sugar, salt, baking powder, and lemon zest. Cut in butter until the mixture resembles coarse crumbs. Mix in pistachios.
c) Add egg and milk, mixing until moistened.
d) Roll out into roughly a 1/2" thick rectangle. Cut in to triangles.
e) Place on an un-greased cookie sheet. Bake for 12-15 min, until golden.
f) Remove scones from the oven and let cool on a wire rack 1-2 minutes before eating.

8. Pistachio Cinnamon Bread

Makes: 2 Loaves

INGREDIENTS:
- 1/2 cup white sugar
- 2 Tablespoons cinnamon
- 1 yellow cake mix
- Two 3.5 ounce boxes of instant pistachio pudding mix
- 4 eggs
- 1/4 cup vegetable oil
- 1/8 cup water
- 1 cup sour cream
- 1 teaspoon green food coloring
- 1 teaspoon vanilla extract
- 1 teaspoon almond extract
- 3 Tablespoons milk
- 1 1/2 cups powdered sugar
- 1/2 cup chopped shelled pistachios

INSTRUCTIONS
a) Preheat oven to 350*F

b) Grease two bread pans with a spray oil or butter.

c) In a small bowl combine white sugar and cinnamon, mix well.

d) Pour cinnamon sugar into loaf pan and gently shake it all around coating the bottom and sides of pan. Coat both pans..

e) In a medium bowl, combine cake mix, pistachio pudding mix, eggs, oil, water & sour cream.

f) Add additional green food coloring if you wish for your bread to be a darker green. Mine is a lime green color, mix well.

g) Batter will be very thick. Pour half the batter into each pan. Spread smoothly on top in preparation for baking.

h) Bake for 45 minutes or until a toothpick inserted into the middle of the bread comes out clean.

i) Let bread rest for 5 minutes before removing from pans and allowing to fully cool on a wire rack.

j) Once cake is fully cooled, make icing.

k) In a small bowl with a hand whisk, combine vanilla extract, almond extract & milk. Mix well.

l) Add powdered sugar 1/2 cup at a time, mixing well after each addition.

m)   After icing is mixed pour over bread.

n) Top immediately with chopped pistachios as icing will dry quickly.

9. Blackberry Pistachio Buns

Makes: 12 buns

INGREDIENTS:
FOR THE BUNS:
- 3 cups all-purpose flour
- 2 cups oat flour
- 1 cup quick cooking oats
- ½ stick unsalted butter, melted
- 1 ½ cups milk, warm
- ¾ cup granulated sugar
- 2 large eggs, room temperature
- 2 tbsp. vanilla sugar
- 1 pouch instant yeast
- 1 tsp. ground cardamom
- ½ tsp. salt
- 2 tbsp. flour for dusting the work surface
- 1 egg, beaten for brushing the dough

FOR THE FILLING:
- 1 ½ cups fresh blackberries
- 1 cup pistachios, crushed
- ⅓ cup granulated sugar

INSTRUCTIONS
FOR THE BUNS:
a) In a large bowl, place the all-purpose flour, oat flour, quick cooking oats, ground cardamom, salt, and whisk them together. Add the granulated sugar, vanilla sugar and instant yeast, and whisk again. Add the eggs, lightly beaten, warm milk, and mix well. Add the melted butter and knead the dough for 5 minutes.

b) Transfer dough into a greased bowl and cover bowl with plastic wrap. Place it in a warm place and let the dough rise until doubled in volume, 1 ½ to 2 hours.

FOR THE FILLING:
c) In a bowl mix together, the blackberries with the sugar.

FOR THE BUNS:

d) Transfer the dough to a floured work surface. Flatten it out with your palm and roll it out into a 30 x 40 cm rectangle. Sprinkle the crushed pistachio, gently pressing down into the dough with your palm. Spread the blackberries, leaving 1 inch border along one long side. Tightly roll the dough and place seam side down making sure to seal the edges as best as you can. Cut 12 equal sections and place them on a on a baking tray lined with parchment paper. Cover the pan with plastic wrap and let them rise for 30 minutes.

e) Preheat oven to 350°F.

f) Brush the buns with beaten egg. Bake them for 40 minutes, or until golden brown.

g) Once baked, let them cool in the baking pan for 5-10 minutes. Transfer to a cooling rack to cool completely.

10. Lemon Doughnuts with Pistachios

INGREDIENTS:

FOR THE DOUGHNUTS:

- Nonstick cooking spray
- 1/2 cup granulated sugar
- Grated zest and juice of 1 lemon
- 1 1/2 cups all-purpose flour
- 3/4 tsp. baking powder
- 1/4 tsp. baking soda
- 1/4 tsp. salt
- 1/3 cup buttermilk
- 1/3 cup whole milk
- 6 Tbs. unsalted butter, at room temperature
- 1 egg
- 2 tsp. vanilla extract

FOR THE GLAZE

- 1/2 cup plain Greek yogurt or other whole milk yogurt
- Grated zest of 1 lemon
- 1/4 tsp. salt
- 1 cup confectioners' sugar
- 1/2 cup toasted pistachios, chopped

INSTRUCTIONS:

a) To make the doughnuts, preheat an oven to 375°F.

b) Coat the wells of a doughnut pan with nonstick cooking spray.

c) In a small bowl, combine the granulated sugar and lemon zest. Using your fingertips, rub the zest into the sugar. In another bowl, whisk together the flour, baking powder, baking soda and salt. In a measuring cup, stir together the buttermilk, whole milk and lemon juice.

d) In the bowl of a stand mixer fitted with the paddle attachment, beat together the sugar mixture and butter on medium speed until light and fluffy, about 2 minutes. Scrape down the sides of the bowl. Add the egg and vanilla and beat on medium speed until combined, about 1 minute.

e) On low speed, add the flour mixture in 3 additions, alternating with the milk mixture and beginning and ending with the flour. Beat each addition until just blended.

f) Pour 2 Tbs. batter into each prepared well. Bake, rotating the pan 180 degrees halfway through baking, until a toothpick inserted into the doughnuts comes out clean, about 10 minutes. Let cool in the pan on a cooling rack for 5 minutes, then invert the doughnuts onto the rack and let cool completely. Meanwhile, wash and dry the pan and repeat to bake the remaining batter.

g) To make the glaze, in a bowl, stir together the yogurt, lemon zest and salt. Add the confectioners' sugar and stir until smooth and well blended. Dip the doughnuts, top side down, into the glaze, sprinkle with the pistachios, and serve. Makes: about sixteen 3-inch doughnuts.

11. Orange Flower, Pistachio, and Date Oatmeal

Makes: 2 servings

INGREDIENTS:
- 1 3/4 cup Plant milk
- 1 cup Old Fashioned Rolled Oats
- 1 pinch salt

TOPPINGS:
- 1/4 cup agave nectar
- 1/2 teaspoon orange flower water
- 1/4 cup chopped pistachios
- 1/4 cup chopped dates
- 1 teaspoon cinnamon

INSTRUCTIONS

a) Bring the plant milk to a boil then add the Old Fashioned Rolled Oats and cook for about 5 minutes or until the oatmeal has absorbed the milk and the oats are tender.

b) Stir in a pinch of salt.

c) Add the orange flower water to the agave nectar and mix well.

d) Divide the cooked oats into 2 bowls and divide the pistachios and dates between them.

e) Drizzle the orange flower water and agave mixture over the top.

f) Top with a sprinkle of cinnamon and enjoy!

12. Pistachios Oatmeal

Makes: 4

INGREDIENTS:
- 2 cups old-fashioned oats
- 2 ¼ cups water
- 2 ¼ cups milk
- ½ teaspoon salt
- ¼ teaspoon nutmeg
- 1 tablespoon honey
- 1 tablespoon dried cranberries
- 1 tablespoon dried cherries
- 1 tablespoon roasted pistachios

INSTRUCTIONS:
a) Add all the ingredients to the Instant Pot, except for cranberries, cherries, and pistachios.
b) Secure the lid of the cooker and press the "Manual" function key.
c) Adjust the time to 6 minutes and cook at high pressure.
d) After the beep, release the pressure naturally and remove the lid.
e) Stir the prepared oatmeal and serve in a bowl.
f) Garnish with cranberries, cherries, and pistachios on top.

13. Golden Waffles with Tropical Fruits

Makes: 4 waffles

INGREDIENTS:
DATE BUTTER
- 1 stick unsalted butter, room temperature
- 1 cup coarsely chopped pitted dates

WAFFLES
- 1 1/2 cups all-purpose flour
- 1 cup coarse-ground semolina flour
- 1/4 cup granulated sugar
- 2 1/2 teaspoons baking powder
- 1/2 teaspoon baking soda
- 3/4 teaspoon coarse salt
- 1 3/4 cup whole milk, room temperature
- 1/3 cup sour cream, room temperature
- 1 stick unsalted butter, melted
- 2 large eggs, room temperature
- 1 teaspoon pure vanilla extract
- Vegetable-oil cooking spray
- Sliced kiwifruits and citrus fruits, chopped pistachios, and pure maple syrup, for serving

INSTRUCTIONS:
Date butter: Pulse butter and dates in a food processor, scraping down sides a few times, until smooth and combined. Date butter can be made up to a week ahead and stored in refrigerator; bring to room temperature before using.

Waffles: Whisk together flours, sugar, baking powder, baking soda, and salt in a large bowl. In a separate bowl, whisk together milk, sour cream, butter, eggs, and vanilla. Whisk milk mixture into flour mixture just to combine.

Preheat a waffle iron. Coat with a thin layer of cooking spray. Pour 1 1/4 cups batter per waffle into center of iron, allowing it to spread almost to edges. Close lid and cook until golden brown and crisp, 6 to 7 minutes. Remove from iron and quickly toss between your hands several times to release steam and help retain crispness, then transfer to a wire rack set in a rimmed baking sheet; keep warm in a 225 degrees oven until ready to serve. Repeat coating iron with more cooking spray between batches. Serve, with date butter, fruit, pistachios, and syrup.

14. Pistachio nut milk

Makes: 4 cups

INGREDIENTS:
- 1 cup dry pistachio nuts
- 4 cups filtered water

INSTRUCTIONS
a) Soak your pistachio nuts for six hours, or overnight.

b) Add the soaked pistachio nuts into a high-speed processor/blender and blend on high.

c) When the nuts are ready, then add the water and blend again for about 1-2 minutes.

d) Pour the liquid into a bowl through layers of cheesecloth or a nut milk bag and squeeze out all the pistachio milk.

e) Stored in the fridge for 3-5 days.

APPETIZERS

15. Pistachio Matcha Balls

Makes: 14 energy balls

INGREDIENTS:
- ½ cup pistachios shelled
- ¾ cup cashews
- 12 dates pitted
- ¼ cup coconut shredded, unsweetened
- 2 teaspoons matcha powder
- 1 tablespoon coconut oil

INSTRUCTIONS:
a) Take ¼ cup pistachios and process in a food processor until finely ground. Remove to a separate bowl and set aside.
b) Add cashews, remaining ¼ cup pistachios, dates, coconut, matcha powder, and coconut oil. Blend well until finely chopped and the mixture is sticky.
c) Scoop mixture out into balls, and roll with hands.
d) Roll balls in ground pistachios and chill for 15 minutes! Enjoy!

16. Parmesan and Ricotta Pizza

Makes: 4 servings

INGREDIENTS:
- Honey Wheat Pizza Dough Recipe
- ¼ Cup Pistachios, Chopped
- 4 Strips of Smoked Bacon, Sliced
- ½ Cup Parmesan cheese, Grated
- 2 Tablespoons Extra Virgin Olive Oil
- ½ teaspoon Pepper, Fresh Ground
- ½ Cup Rainbow mix Micro Greens
- ¼ teaspoon Sea Salt
- ½ Cup Ricotta Cheese

INSTRUCTIONS:
a) Preheat oven to 500 degrees Fahrenheit.
b) In a mixing bowl, combine the Ricotta, Parmesan, Olive Oil, Sea Salt, and Pepper. Stir thoroughly.
c) Cover the prepared pizza dough with the filling.
d) Place half of the pistachios on top, then layer the bacon.
e) Bake for 16 minutes, or until the bacon is crisp and the dough is golden brown.
f) Garnish with the remaining pistachios and microgreens.

17. Lentil, pistachio, and shiitake burger

Makes: 4 servings

INGREDIENTS:
FOR THE BURGERS
- 3 shallots, diced
- 2 teaspoons olive oil
- ½ cup black lentils, rinsed
- 6 dried shiitake mushroom caps
- ½ cup pistachios
- ¼ cup fresh parsley, chopped
- ¼ cup vital wheat gluten
- 1 Tablespoon Ener-G, whisked with ⅛ cup water
- 2 teaspoons dried rubbed sage
- ½ teaspoon salt
- ¼ teaspoon cracked pepper

FOR THE FRIES
- 3 potatoes, peeled and thinly cut
- vegetable oil, for frying
- salt

INSTRUCTIONS
a) Bring three cups of water to a boil. While you are waiting for the water to heat up, throw the diced shallots into a separate sauté pan with the oil and sauté over low heat.

b) When the water starts to boil, add in the lentils and dried shiitake caps and place the cover over the pot so some steam can escape during cooking. Boil for 18-20 minutes, then pour them into a fine-mesh strainer to drain and cool. Once cooled, remove the shiitake from the lentils and dice them up, discarding the tough stems.

c) Place the pistachios into a food processor and coarsely grind them. By this time, your shallots should be nicely caramelized. Add the shallots, lentils, diced shiitake caps, pistachios, and parsley to a bowl and mix until well combined. Add in the vital wheat gluten and stir.

d) Now add in the water/Energ-G mixture and stir for about two minutes with a strong fork to allow the gluten to develop. Now add in the sage and salt and pepper and stir until well combined. You can then either place the mixture in the refrigerator for a few hours or fry the burgers immediately.

e) To fry the burgers, shape them into patties, slightly squeezing the mixture together as you are shaping it. Fry in a sauté pan with a little olive oil for 2-3 minutes on each side, or until it is slightly browned.

f) To make the fries, place several inches of vegetable oil in a pot. Heat over high heat.

g) Fry in batches.

h) Fry until crisp, about 4-5 minutes, and remove from the oil with heat-resistant tongs.

i) Transfer to paper towels to drain and sprinkle immediately with a little salt.

18. Baklava

INGREDIENTS:

- 3½ cup sugar
- 2½ cup water
- 2 tablespoons honey
- 2 teaspoons lemon juice
- 1 stick cinnamon
- 3 whole cloves
- ½ pound Walnuts, finely ground
- ½ pound almonds, finely ground
- ½ pound pistachios, finely ground
- 2 teaspoons ground cinnamon
- ½ teaspoon cloves
- 1½ pounds Phyllo pastry
- 1 pound/4 sticks unsalted butter, melted

INSTRUCTIONS:

a) In a saucepan, combine;

b) 3 cups sugar with the water, honey, lemon juice, cinnamon stick, and cloves and let it cool.

c) In a large bowl, combine the nuts, remaining ½ cup sugar, ground cinnamon, and ground cloves. Set aside.

d) Unroll phyllo dough on a flat surface and keep covered with wax paper or a damp towel.

e) Remove 8 sheets and put them in the refrigerator.

f) Using a pastry brush, brush a 15½x11 ½ x 3 baking pan with melted butter,

g) Use 8 sheets for the bottom and sprinkle with the nuts mixture.

h) Layer 3 more sheets and sprinkle with the mixture again. Continue until all the phyllo is used.

i) Top with 8 sheets.

j) Preheat oven to 300 degrees F.

k) Using a long and very sharp knife, cut the baklava into small diamonds.

l) First, make 1 evenly spaced lengthwise cuts.

m) Cut straight down in a line and cut diagonally across the lengthwise cuts.

n) Heat the remaining butter and pour it over the top of the baklava,

o) Bake for 1¼ hours.

p) Remove and spoon the cooled syrup over the entire pastry in the pan.

q) Serve in decorative cups.

19. Pistachio caramels

Makes: 48 pieces

INGREDIENTS:
- ½ cup butter
- 2 cups dark brown sugar
- ½ cup dark corn syrup
- 2 cups heavy cream
- ¼ tsp. salt
- 1 cup chopped pistachios, roasted
- 2 tsp. vanilla extract

INSTRUCTIONS
a) Line an 8-inch square pan with aluminum foil, spray with nonstick cooking spray, and set aside.

b) In a medium saucepan over low heat, melt butter. Add dark brown sugar, dark corn syrup, 1 cup heavy cream, and salt. Bring to a boil, stirring occasionally, for 12 to 15 minutes or until mixture reaches 225°F on a candy thermometer.

c) Slowly add remaining 1 cup heavy cream. Bring mixture to a boil and cook for 15 more minutes or until it reaches 250°F.

d) Remove from heat and add pistachios and vanilla extract. Pour into the prepared pan.

e) Cool for at least 3 hours before removing from the foil and cutting into 48 pieces.

f) Cut wax paper into 48 3-inch squares. Place each caramel in the center of a wax paper square, roll up the paper around caramel, and twist the ends of the paper.

20. Chocolate-dipped nougatine

Makes: 12 pieces

INGREDIENTS:
- ¾ cup granulated sugar
- ⅓ cup light corn syrup
- ¼ cup chopped pistachios
- ¾ cup sliced almonds
- 2 Tablespoon butter
- 1 cup dark chocolate chips

INSTRUCTIONS

a) Line a baking sheet with parchment paper and set aside. In a medium saucepan over medium heat, stir sugar and light corn syrup for 5 to 7 minutes until mixture is melted and starting to caramelize.

b) Mix in pistachios, almonds, and butter, and stir for 2 to 3 minutes to lightly toast almonds.

c) Transfer nougatine mixture onto the prepared baking sheet and top with an additional sheet of parchment paper. Spread evenly with a rolling pin until about ½ inch thick. Cut into 12 pieces.

d) In a double boiler over medium heat, heat dark chocolate chips for 5 to 7 minutes or until melted.

e) Dip nougatine pieces into melted chocolate, covering just half of nougatine, and return to the parchment-lined baking sheet. Allow chocolate to set for at least 1 hour.

f) Storage: Keep in an airtight container for up to 1 week.

21. Pistachio crunch

Makes: 2 Cups

INGREDIENTS:
- 75 g pistachios, raw, unsalted [½ cup]
- 155 g pistachio paste [½ cup]
- 60 g feuilletine [¾ cup]
- 40 g confectioners' sugar [¼ cup]
- 4 g kosher salt [1 teaspoon]

INSTRUCTIONS
a) Heat the oven to 325°F.

b) Put the pistachios on a sheet pan and toast in the oven for 15 minutes. Cool to room temperature.

c) Put the toasted pistachios in a clean kitchen towel and, with a sauté pan or a rolling pin, bash them into smaller pieces, ideally halving the pistachios, or breaking them down to no smaller than one-eighth their original size.

d) Combine the broken pistachios with the pistachio paste, feuilletine, confectioners' sugar, and salt in the bowl of a stand mixer fitted with the paddle attachment and paddle on medium-low speed for about 1 minute, until homogeneous. The crunch can be stored in an airtight container at room temperature for 5 days or in the fridge for up to 2 weeks.

22. Pistachio sugar cookies

Makes: 1 serving

INGREDIENTS:
- ½ cup Butter
- 1 cup Sugar
- 1 large Egg
- 1 teaspoon Vanilla
- 1¼ cup Sifted flour
- 1 teaspoon Baking powder
- ¼ teaspoon Salt
- ⅓ cup Finely chopped pistachios

INSTRUCTIONS

a) In a large bowl, cream butter and sugar until soft and fluffy; beat in egg and vanilla. Combine flour, baking powder and salt; add to creamed mixture and mix well. Chill dough thoroughly.

b) Preheat oven to 375ø. Roll dough out to ¼-inch thick on lightly floured board. Cut with cookie cutters and arrange on ungreased cookie sheets. Sprinkle chopped pistachios on top; press down lightly.

c) Bake at 375ø for about 5 minutes or until edges start to brown.

d) Remove to wire racks to cool.

23. Pistachio & white chocolate cookies

Makes: 36 servings

INGREDIENTS:
- 1¼ cup Firmly packed light brown
- Sugar
- ¾ cup Butter flavored crisco
- 2 tablespoons Milk
- 1 teaspoon Vanilla
- 1 Egg
- 1¾ cup Flour
- 1 teaspoon Salt
- ¾ teaspoon Baking soda
- 1 cup White chocolate chunks
- 1 cup Pistachios, toasted, skinned, and Chopped

INSTRUCTIONS

a) Preheat oven to 375F. Place sheets of foil wrap on cooling surface.

b) Beat brown sugar, crisco, milk and vanilla until well blended, then beat in egg.

c) Combine flour, soda and salt then add to creamed mixture just until blended. Stir in white chocolate and nuts gently.

d) Drop by teaspoonfuls 3" apart on ungreased cookie sheets. Bake, one sheet at a time, about 8-10 minutes for chewy or 11-13 minutes for crisp cookies.

e) Cool on sheet 2 minutes, remove to foil.

24. Pistachio wafers

Makes: 1 serving

INGREDIENTS:
- 3 eaches Egg whites
- pinch Of salt
- ⅓ cup Castor sugar
- 1 cup Plain flour
- 150 grams Pistachio nuts, shelled
- 1 teaspoon Orange flower or rose water

INSTRUCTIONS
a) Whisk egg whites with salt until they form stiff peaks.
b) Add sugar gradually and whisk until shiny.
c) Fold in flour, pistachios and rose water.
d) Grease and flour a loaf tin and spoon in mixture.
e) Bake for 35 to 40 minutes in pre-heated 180'C oven.
f) Turn out, cool and wrap in foil. Refrigerate overnight. Slice finely and place slices on baking tray.
g) Allow to dry out in a cool oven. Wafers should be crisp. Store in an airtight container.

25. Pistachio Muffins

Makes: 12 muffins

INGREDIENTS:
- 2 cups all-purpose flour, spooned and leveled
- 1 3.4-oz box instant pistachio pudding mix, dry
- 2 teaspoon baking powder
- ¾ teaspoon salt
- ½ cup neutral-tasting oil
- 8 oz buttermilk
- ¾ cup granulated sugar
- 2 eggs
- 1 teaspoon vanilla extract
- ½ teaspoon almond extract
- ½ cup unsalted pistachios, chopped

INSTRUCTIONS
a) Preheat oven to 350°F. Line a 12-cup regular muffin tin with muffin cups. Lightly spritz the tin and papers with cooking spray. This helps the muffin papers peel back cleanly.

b) Whisk together flour, dry instant pudding mix, baking powder, and salt in a mixing bowl. Set aside for now.

c) In a separate bowl, add oil, buttermilk, sugar, eggs, vanilla extract, and almond extract. Using a hand or stand mixer, beat 1-2 minutes until light and creamy.

d) Pour in dry ingredients and mix until just combined. Fold in chopped pistachios, taking care not to overmix the batter.

e) Evenly transfer the batter to the prepared muffin tin. I like to use a cookie scoop to cut down on drips and mess.

f) Bake for 18-20 minutes, or until a thin tester inserted into the tallest part of a muffin comes out clean.

g) If using muffin papers, immediately remove the muffins from the pan and let them cool completely on a wire rack. This helps prevent condensation from sogging up the papers. If you're not using muffin papers, you can leave the muffins in the pan for 5-10 minutes, before carefully loosening the edges and transferring to a wire rack to cool completely.

h) Store muffins in an air-tight container only after they have completely cooled. Lightly pressing a paper towel along the top of the muffins in their storage container will absorb excess moisture that forms after a few days.

26. Black Olive And Pesto Pizza

Makes: 4 SERVINGS

CRUST
1 recipe Buckwheat Pizza Crust, Tomato Pizza Crust, Oregano Pizza Crust, or Instant Pizza Crust
TOPPINGS
1 recipe Avocado-Pistachio Pesto
1 tomato, sliced and seeded
3 tablespoons thinly sliced red onion
½ cup diced and seeded green bell pepper
¼ cup pitted, chopped black olives
1 recipe Rawmesan Cheese or Cheezy Sprinkle
Olive oil or Herb-Infused Olive Oil

To assemble your pizza, spread the pesto on the pizza crust. Top with the tomato and onion slices, then sprinkle with the bell pepper, olives, and Rawmesan Cheese.
Drizzle a few tablespoons of olive oil over your pizza just before serving, to create that baked pizza greasy-mouth feel when you bite into it.
Will keep for a couple of days in the fridge.

27. Pears Puff Pastry Pinwheels

Makes: 25 pinwheels

INGREDIENTS:
- 1 sheet puff pastry dough thawed
- ⅔ cup pear cut into very small cubes
- ¼ cup Asiago cheese I use Peppered Asiago Cheese, shredded
- ⅛ cups pistachios finely chopped
- ⅛ cup dried cranberries finely chopped
- ½ teaspoon rosemary optional
- 1 egg, beaten
- ½ teaspoon sea salt

INSTRUCTIONS:
a) On a floured surface, unfold the thawed puff pastry and roll into a larger square, mainly to make the pastry sheet thinner.

b) On a large cutting board, prepare the fillings. Cut the pear in half and remove the core. Slice the pear into thin slices and then cut the slices into stripes and then dice.

c) Using a grater, shred the cheese, or you can use preshredded cheese.

d) In a small bowl beat the egg. Top the dough with the all the filling Leave one long side of the pastry without the filling and brush with the beaten egg.

e) Start rolling the pastry over the ingredients into a tight roll.Seal the edge with the beaten egg.

f) Heat the oven to 400° F while the pastry is chillig.

g) Wrap the logs in plastic and chill in the refrigerator for an hour. Or at this point, you can freeze these rolls for several months.

h) After the pastry is chilled, cut into slices. I cut mine into ½" slices.Place on a baking sheet lined with a silcon baking mat. Brush the top with the egg wash and sprinkle with salt.

i) Bake the pastries for 17-20 minutes until lightly golden brown.

j) These pastries are best served while warm.

k) Store any leftover pastries in an airtight container.

MAIN COURSE

28. Curried Rice Pistachio Pilaf

Makes:s: 4

INGREDIENTS:
- 1 cup long grain white rice
- 1 cup frozen peas
- 1 medium onion
- ¼ cup roasted unsalted pistachios
- 3 garlic cloves
- 2 tablespoons Coconut oil
- 1½ teaspoons curry powder
- ½ bunch cilantro tough stems removed
- lime
- Kosher salt
- Freshly ground black pepper

INSTRUCTIONS
a) Peel and finely chop 1 onion and 4 garlic cloves.

b) Heat Coconut oil in a Dutch oven over medium heat. Cook onion and garlic until translucent and fragrant. Season with salt and pepper.

c) Add rice and stir until everything is evenly combined and the grains are completely coated. Sauté for 3-5 minutes or until the grains become translucent.

d) Stir in curry powder and sauté for 1 minute until toasted.

e) Add water and stir, making sure to scrape the bottom of the pan for the crispy bits. Bring to boil and reduce to simmer.

f) Let rice steam until water is absorbed and grains are tender, 12–15 minutes. Remove pot from heat, uncover, and stir in 1 cup frozen peas. Place lid on top and let rice continue to gently steam about 5 minutes

g) While pilaf is resting, coarsely chop ½ bunch cilantro and ¼ cup pistachios. Cut 1 lime into wedges.

h) Remove lid and towel and fluff rice with a fork. Season with more salt and pepper and stir in pistachios and cilantro.

i) Transfer to a serving bowl. Serve with lime wedges.

29. Tofu with Pistachio-Pomegranate Sauce

Makes: 4 servings

INGREDIENTS:
- 1 pound extra-firm tofu, drained, cut into ¼-inch slices, and pressed
- Salt and freshly ground black pepper
- 2 tablespoons olive oil
- ½ cup pomegranate juice
- 1 tablespoon balsamic vinegar
- 1 tablespoon light brown sugar
- 2 green onions, minced
- ½ cup unsalted shelled pistachios, coarsely chopped
- Season the tofu with salt and pepper to taste.

INSTRUCTIONS

a) In a large skillet, heat the oil over medium heat. Add the tofu slices, in batches if necessary, and cook until lightly browned, about 4 minutes per side. Remove from skillet and set aside.

b) In the same skillet, add the pomegranate juice, vinegar, sugar, and green onions and simmer over medium heat, for 5 minutes. Add half of the pistachios and cook until sauce is slightly thickened, about 5 minutes.

c) Return the fried tofu to the skillet and cook until hot, about 5 minutes, spooning the sauce over the tofu as it simmers. Serve immediately, sprinkled with the remaining pistachios.

30. Buttercup Squash Stuffed With Pistachio-Apricot Rice

Makes: 4 servings

INGREDIENTS:
- 1 large buttercup squash, halved crosswise and seeded
- 2 tablespoons olive oil
- 1 large yellow onion, chopped
- 1 cup brown basmati rice
- Salt
- 2 cups water
- ½ cup dried apricots, minced
- ½ cup chopped unsalted shelled pistachios
- 3 tablespoons minced fresh cilantro
- 1 teaspoon ground coriander
- Freshly ground black pepper

INSTRUCTIONS

a) Preheat the oven to 375°F. Lightly oil a 9 x 13-inch baking pan and set aside. Place the squash halves, cut side down, in the prepared baking pan. Add $\frac{1}{4}$ inch of water, cover tightly, and bake until almost tender, about 30 minutes.

b) In a large saucepan, heat the oil over medium heat. Add the onion, cover, and cook until tender, about 5 minutes. Add the rice, salt to taste, and water and bring to a boil. Cover, reduce heat to low, and simmer until the rice is cooked, about 30 minutes. Remove from the heat and set aside.

c) Remove the squash halves from the oven and carefully turn them over, cut side up.

d) Fluff the rice with a fork and add the apricots, pistachios, cilantro, and coriander. Season with salt and pepper to taste. Divide the stuffing between the squash halves, packing tightly. Cover with foil and bake until hot, 20 to 30 minutes. Serve immediately.

31. Pistachio baked fish

Makes: 5 Servings

INGREDIENTS:
- 1 pounds Fresh or frozen fish fillets
- ½ cup Dry bread crumbs
- ½ cup Chopped shelled pistachios
- 2 tablespoons Grated Parmesan cheese
- 1 tablespoon Minced parsley
- 1 teaspoon Dry mustard
- Salt and pepper to taste
- ¼ cup Milk
- 2 tablespoons Butter or margarine,melted

INSTRUCTIONS
a) Cut fish into serving size pieces.
b) Combine bread crumbs,¼ cup pistachios,cheese,parsley,mustard,salt and pepper in a shallow dish.
c) Dip fish in milk and roll in crumb mixture;place in a shallow greased baking dish.
d) Drizzle with butter;sprinkle with remaining pistachios.

32. Pistachio and chicken terrine

Makes: 1 serving

INGREDIENTS:
- ⅓ pounds Asparagus spears
- 2¼ pounds Boneless skinless chicken
- 2 Eggs
- 2 cups Heavy cream
- 1 teaspoon Salt
- ½ teaspoon Pepper
- 1 cup Shelled unsalted pistachio
- Nuts

INSTRUCTIONS

a) Preheat oven to 325. Blanch asparagus. Drain & dry. Process chicken until very smooth.

b) Add eggs, cream, salt & pepper. blend well. Stir in nuts by hand. Line 9"X5" pan with foil.

c) Leave a little foil over edges. Butter. Pour ½ chicken mixture. Lay vegetables on top.

d) Pour in remaining chicken mixture. Place buttered wax paper on top.

e) Place in large pan with 1½" water. Bake 40 minutes.

f) Remove. Weigh lightly 2 hours. Chill. Unmold & serve.

33. Pistachio encrusted salmon with beurre blanc

Makes: 1 serving

INGREDIENTS:
- 6 Salmon fillets
- 1 cup Pistachios; shelled and finely ground
- ½ cup White wine
- Lemon juice of 1 1/2 lemons
- Lemon zest; to taste
- ¼ pounds Cold butter; cubed
- Chives

INSTRUCTIONS:
a) Pat salmon in ground pistachios, then sear both sides in hot skillet until nuts are golden.

b) Finish in a 400 oven until done.

FOR THE BEURRE BLANC

c) Reduce wine, lemon juice and shallots in a skillet.

d) Whisk in lemon zest and cold butter.

e) Add chives just before serving.

f) Pour over salmon and serve immediately.

g) Garnish with lemon twist and chives.

h) Serve with basmati rice and fresh vegetables.

34. Gnocchetti with shrimp & pesto

Makes: 4–6

INGREDIENTS:
- Semolina Dough

PISTACHIO PESTO
- 1 cup pistachios
- 1 bunch mint
- 1 garlic clove
- ½ cup grated Pecorino Romano
- ½ cup olive oil
- Kosher salt
- Freshly ground black pepper
- 8 oz fava beans
- Olive oil
- 3 garlic cloves, chopped
- 2 lb large shrimp, cleaned
- Crushed red pepper, to taste
- Kosher salt
- Freshly ground black pepper
- ¼ cup white wine
- 1 lemon, zested

INSTRUCTIONS

a) Dust two sheet pans with semolina flour.

b) To make the gnocchetti, cut off a small piece of dough and cover the rest of the dough with plastic wrap. With your hands, roll the piece of dough into a rope about ½-inch thick. Cut ½-inch pieces of dough from the rope. With your thumb, gently push the piece of dough onto a gnocchi board, rolling it away from your body so it creates a slight indentation. Place the gnocchetti on the semolina-dusted sheet pans and leave it uncovered until ready to cook.

c) To make the pistachio pesto, in a food processor, add the pistachios, mint, garlic, Pecorino Romano, olive oil, salt and freshly ground black pepper, and process until puréed.

d) Prepare a bowl of ice water. Remove the fava beans from the pod. Blanch the fava beans by cooking them in boiling water until tender, about 1 minute. Remove from the water and place in the ice bath. When cool enough, remove from the water and set aside in a bowl. Remove the waxy outer layer of the bean and discard.

e) Bring a large pot of salted water to a boil. In the meantime, in a large sauté pan over high heat, add a drizzle of olive oil, garlic, shrimp, crushed red pepper, salt and freshly ground black pepper. While the shrimp are cooking, drop the pasta in the boiling water and cook until al dente, about 3 to 4 minutes. Add the pasta to the sauté pan with white wine and let cook until wine is reduced by half, about a minute.

f) To serve, divide the pasta between bowls. Garnish with lemon zest and pistachio pesto.

35. Pistachio Crusted Lamb Chops

Makes: 4

INGREDIENTS:
- 1 tbsp. olive oil
- 1 tsp. fine sea salt
- Freshly ground black pepper
- ½ tsp. ground cumin
- ¼ cup fresh shredded Parmesan cheese
- ¼ cup parsley leaves
- ¼ tsp. garlic powder
- ½ cup raw shelled pistachios
- 2 large egg whites, lightly beaten
- 1 lamb rack, French trimmed and cut into 8 individual chops

INSTRUCTIONS:
a) Preheat oven to 400 degrees. Line a large sheet tray with a wire rack.
b) Combine the cumin, parmesan cheese, parsley and garlic powder in the bowl of a food processor and pulse about 30 seconds, until everything is thoroughly combined. Add in the pistachios and pulse until the pistachios are finely chopped. Taste and adjust seasoning as needed.
c) In a medium bowl, lightly beat the egg whites.
d) Pat each lamb chop dry and season with salt and pepper. Dip each lamb chop in the egg mixture, shake off excess, and then dip the chop into the pistachio crumb mixture making sure all sides are fully coated. Heat 1 tablespoon of olive oil over medium-high heat in a large cast iron skillet.
e) Sear each lamb chop for about 3 minutes on each side or until golden brown.
f) Transfer the lamb chops to the prepared sheet tray and roast for 3-5 minutes in the oven.
g) Serve immediately.

36. Crispy Pistachio Chicken With Zucchini Ribbon Salad

Makes: 4

INGREDIENTS:
PISTACHIO CHICKEN
- 1 pound boneless, skinless chicken breasts
- 1 cup chopped pistachios
- ¾ cup seasoned breadcrumbs
- ⅔ cup freshly grated parmesan cheese
- 1 teaspoon garlic powder
- kosher salt and pepper
- 2 large eggs, lightly beaten

ZUCCHINI RIBBON SALAD
- 2 medium zucchini
- 1 lemon, freshly squeezed
- 1 garlic clove, minced
- 2 tablespoons finely grated parmesan cheese
- ¼ cup extra virgin olive oil
- shaved parmesan cheese, for topping

INSTRUCTIONS
a) Preheat the oven to 425 degrees Line a baking sheet with aluminum foil and place a wire rack on top. Spray the rack with nonstick spray and set aside.

b) Pound the chicken with a meat tenderizer until it is about ¼ to ½ inch in thickness. Season the chicken well on both sides with salt and pepper.

c) In a small bowl, lightly beat the eggs. In a large bowl, combine the pistachios, breadcrumbs, garlic powder and parmesan cheese. Dip each piece of chicken in the beaten egg and then dredge it through the bread crumbs, pressing lightly to adhere.

d) Place the chicken pieces on the wire rack. Spray each with a mist of olive oil/grapeseed oil/coconut oil.

e) Bake the chicken for 10 to 12 minutes, remove it from the oven, gently flip each piece and mist with spray, then bake for 10 to 12 minutes more.

f) Let the chicken rest for 5 to 10 minutes before slicing.

g) While the chicken bakes, make the zucchini ribbon salad! Use a vegetable peeler to slice ribbons from a zucchini lengthwise. Place them in a bowl.

h) Whisk together the lemon juice, garlic, parmesan and olive oil with a big pinch of salt and pepper. Drizzle it over the zucchini ribbons and toss. Top with shaved parmesan. Serve with the crispy pistachio chicken!

37. Pistachio-Crusted Halibut

Makes: 4 servings

INGREDIENTS:
- 2 Tbsp . Dijon mustard
- 1 tsp . finely grated lemon peel
- 1 dash sea salt
- Ground black pepper
- 4 raw halibut fillets
- ¼ cup raw , unsalted pistachios, finely chopped
- 1 Tbsp . corn meal
- 1 Tbsp . finely chopped parsley

INSTRUCTIONS
a) Preheat oven to 400° F.

b) Combine mustard, lemon peel, salt, and pepper in a small bowl; mix well.

c) Spread mustard mixture evenly on top side of each halibut fillet. Set aside.

d) Combine pistachios, corn meal, and parsley in a medium bowl; mix well.

e) Press pistachio mixture evenly into top side of each halibut fillet.

f) Place halibut in baking dish, pistachio side up. Bake for 8 to10 minutes, or until halibut flakes easily when tested with a fork.

38. Roast Fillet of Beef Stuffed with Mortadella & Pistachio Nuts

Makes: 6-8

INGREDIENTS:
- 2¼ pounds piece trimmed grass-fed fillet of beef, of an even thickness, at room temperature
- 3½ ounces thinly sliced mortadella, or ham off the bone, finely chopped
- 3 cloves garlic, peeled and crushed
- ¼ tsp freshly grated nutmeg
- 2 Tbsp panko crumbs or fresh white breadcrumbs
- 1 tsp flaky sea salt, plus extra for sprinkling
- ½ tsp freshly ground black pepper
- 1 small free-range egg, lightly beaten
- 1 cup, loosely packed, basil leaves
- 20 toasted pistachio nuts, shelled
- 2 Tbsp olive oil
- 3 Tbsp full-bodied red wine

INSTRUCTIONS:
a) Preheat oven to 410°F, setting a shelf in the middle of the oven. Rinse fillet and pat dry.

b) Remove any fat and silverskin. Make a small cut in the centre of the meat with a sharp pointy knife, then use the rounded handle of a wooden spoon to push through the meat to form a small tunnel.

c) Mix the mortadella, garlic, nutmeg, crumbs, salt and pepper together in a small bowl. Add enough egg to bind.

d) Stuff into the cavity in the fillet, using the wooden spoon to help push it in, threading in the basil as you go and adding the pistachio nuts.

e) Tie the fillet into a good shape with string. If it has become moist, pat dry with paper towels again to minimize spitting once it goes in the oil. Heat the oil in a shallow but sturdy roasting tin over a medium-high heat. When the oil is nice and hot, lower in the fillet and turn it quickly in the hot oil, then let it brown on one side for 2 minutes. No more!

f) Turn fillet over again with tongs and immediately transfer to a hot oven. Cook meat for 6 minutes, remove from oven, turn it over again and return to the oven.

g) For rare to medium-rare meat, cook for a further 5-6 minutes, or until the internal temperature of the thickest part of the meat reaches 110°F, or until it is done to your liking.

h) Remove meat from oven, spoon over any juices, then season generously on all sides with salt. Rest beef for 12-15 minutes before slicing.

i) Remove string from meat, then slice it evenly. Let meat rest a minute or two before transferring to a heated serving platter. Skim pan juices, pour in wine and let it bubble up briefly. Spoon juices over meat and serve immediately.

39. Roast chicken with pistachio pesto

Makes: 4-6

INGREDIENTS:
- 25g shelled pistachios
- 1 large bunch fresh basil, leaves and stalks roughly chopped
- 4 fresh mint sprigs, leaves roughly chopped
- Grated zest and juice ½ lemon, plus ½ lemon
- 125ml extra-virgin olive oil
- 2kg whole free-range chicken
- 125ml dry white wine
- 200g sourdough bread, torn into chunks
- 200g mixed radishes, halved or quartered if large
- 250g asparagus
- Large handful pea shoots
- Useful but not essentia

INSTRUCTIONS:

a) Heat the oven to 200°C/180°C fan/gas 6. Whizz the pistachios, basil, mint and lemon zest and juice in a mini chopper or small food processor to a rough paste. Drizzle in 100ml oil, then season and whizz to combine. Put half the pesto in a small serving dish and set aside.

b) Put the chicken in a large shallow roasting tin. Working from the neck cavity, use your fingers to make a pocket between the skin and flesh

c) of the breasts. Push the pesto under the skin of the chicken and rub any excess over the skin. Squeeze the remaining ½ lemon over the chicken, then place in the cavity. Roast for 20 minutes, then turn the oven down to 190°C/170°C fan/gas 5.

d) Add the wine and 125ml water to the tin and roast for 40-50 minutes more until the chicken is cooked through.

e) Put the chicken on a board, cover loosely with foil and set aside to rest. Pour the roasting juices from the tin into a jug. Add the bread, radishes and asparagus to the roasting tin, spoon off some of the fat from the top of the juices and toss it with the bread and vegetables.

f) Season, then roast for 12-15 minutes until the veg are tender and the bread is crisp. Discard any fat from the remaining juices and warm in a pan for a gravy.

g) Mix the remaining pesto and 25ml olive oil and drizzle over the chicken and veg. Serve with the pea shoots and gravy on the side.

40. Saffron Rice with Barberries, Pistachio & Mixed Herbs

Makes: 6

2½ tbsp / 40 g unsalted butter

2 cups / 360 g basmati rice, rinsed under cold water and drained well

2⅓ cups / 560 ml boiling water

1 tsp saffron threads, soaked in 3 tbsp boiling water for 30 minutes

¼ cup / 40 g dried barberries, soaked for a few minutes in boiling water with a pinch of sugar

1 oz / 30 g dill, coarsely chopped

⅔ oz / 20 g chervil, coarsely chopped

⅓ oz / 10 g tarragon, coarsely chopped

½ cup / 60 g slivered or crushed unsalted pistachios, lightly toasted

salt and freshly ground white pepper

Melt the butter in a medium saucepan and stir in the rice, making sure the grains are well coated in butter. Add the boiling water, 1 teaspoon salt, and some white pepper. Mix well, cover with a tightly fitting lid, and leave to cook over very low heat for 15 minutes. Don't be tempted to uncover the pan; you'll need to allow the rice to steam properly.

Remove the rice pan from the heat—all the water will have been absorbed by the rice—and pour the saffron water over one side of the rice, covering about one-quarter of the surface and leaving the majority of it white. Cover the pan immediately with a tea towel and reseal tightly with the lid. Set aside for 5 to 10 minutes.

Use a large spoon to remove the white part of the rice into a large mixing bowl and fluff it up with a fork. Drain the barberries and stir them in, followed by the herbs and most of the pistachios, leaving a few to garnish. Mix well. Fluff the saffron rice with a fork and gently fold it into the white rice. Don't overmix—you don't want the white grains to be stained by the yellow. Taste and adjust the seasoning. Transfer the rice to a shallow serving bowl and scatter the remaining pistachios on top. Serve warm or at room temperature.

41. Braised Eggs with Lamb, Tahini & Sumac

Makes: 4

1 tbsp olive oil

1 large onion, finely chopped (1¼ cups / 200 g in total)

6 cloves garlic, sliced thinly

10 oz / 300 g ground lamb

2 tsp sumac, plus extra to finish

1 tsp ground cumin

½ cup / 50 g toasted unsalted pistachios, crushed

7 tbsp / 50 g toasted pine nuts

2 tsp harissa paste (store-bought or see recipe)

1 tbsp finely chopped preserved lemon peel (store-bought or see recipe)

1⅓ cups / 200 g cherry tomatoes

½ cup / 120 ml chicken stock

4 large free-range eggs

¼ cup / 5 g picked cilantro leaves, or 1 tbsp Zhoug

salt and freshly ground black pepper

YOGURT SAUCE

½ cup / 100 g Greek yogurt

1½ tbsp / 25 g tahini paste

2 tbsp freshly squeezed lemon juice

1 tbsp water

Heat the olive oil over medium-high heat in a medium, heavy-bottomed frying pan for which you have a tight-fitting lid. Add the onion and garlic and sauté for 6 minutes to soften and color a bit. Raise the heat to high, add the lamb, and brown well, 5 to 6 minutes. Season with the sumac, cumin, ¾ teaspoon salt, and some black pepper and cook for another minute. Turn off the heat, stir in the nuts, harissa, and preserved lemon and set aside.

While the onion is cooking, heat a separate small cast-iron or other heavy pan over high heat. Once piping hot, add the cherry tomatoes and char for 4 to 6 minutes, tossing them in the pan occasionally, until slightly blackened on the outside. Set aside.

Prepare the yogurt sauce by whisking together all the ingredients with a pinch of salt. It needs to be thick and rich, but you may need to add a splash of water if it is stiff.

You can leave the meat, tomatoes, and sauce at this stage for up to an hour. When you are ready to serve, reheat the meat, add the chicken stock, and bring to a boil. Make 4 small wells in the mix and break an egg into each well. Cover the pan and cook the eggs over low heat for 3 minutes. Place the tomatoes on top, avoiding the yolks, cover again, and cook for 5 minutes, until the egg whites are cooked but the yolks are still runny.

Remove from the heat and dot with dollops of the yogurt sauce, sprinkle with sumac, and finish with the cilantro. Serve at once.

42. Salmon with Bailey's Irish Cream Sauce

Makes: 4 servings

INGREDIENTS:
FOR THE SALMON:
- 4 salmon fillets, 6-8 ounces each
- 2 tablespoons whole grain mustard, plus 1 teaspoon for the sauce
- ½ cup shelled raw pistachios
- ¼ cup toasted bread crumbs

FOR THE SAUCE:
- 1 tablespoon butter
- 1 tablespoon shallot, peeled and finely diced
- 2 cups heavy cream
- ¼ cup Bailey's Irish Cream
- 4 thyme sprigs, for garnish

PREPARE THE SALMON:
a) Toast the pistachios in a dry pan over medium heat until fragrant and lightly toasted. Be careful not to burn them, as nuts have a high oil content, and can go from toasted to burnt really quickly.
b) Grind the pistachios to a medium fine texture by pulsing gently in a food processor.
c) Mix with the bread crumbs.
d) Coat the top of each salmon fillet with mustard and press into the pistachio and bread crumb mixture to coat. Heat a large skillet over high heat, and add the remaining olive oil. Sear the salmon fillets, pistachio side down, over medium-high heat, until a crust has formed, about 2-3 minutes.
e) Gently turn the fillets over and sear on the second side for an additional 2 minutes. Remove the fillets from the pan, place them in an oven safe dish, and bake in the oven with the cabbage slaw for 20 minutes.
MAKE THE SAUCE:

f) Wipe the skillet with a paper towel, then melt the butter over medium-high heat. Add the shallots, and sauté them lightly.

g) When shallots are translucent and fragrant, add the heavy cream and Bailey's Irish Cream. Reduce until the sauce thickens.

h) Whisk the remaining teaspoon mustard into the sauce and season with salt and pepper to taste.

43. Rainbow Chard with Goji Berries and Pistachios

Makes: 4 servings

INGREDIENTS:
- 2 tablespoons olive oil
- 1 small red onion, minced
- 2 garlic cloves, minced
- 1 bunch of rainbow chard, finely chopped
- Salt and freshly ground black pepper
- ⅓ cup goji berries
- ⅓ cup unsalted shelled pistachios

INSTRUCTIONS:
a) In a large skillet, heat the oil over medium heat. Add the onion, cover, and cook until softened, about 5 minutes. Add the garlic and cook, stirring, to soften For 30 seconds.

b) Add the chard and cook, stirring until wilted, 3 to 4 minutes. Season with salt and pepper to taste and cook, uncovered, stirring occasionally, until tender, about 5 to 7 minutes.

c) Add the goji berries and pistachios and toss to combine. Serve immediately.

44. Heirloom tomato and nectarine salad

Makes: 6

INGREDIENTS:
- ¼ cup extra-virgin olive oil
- 3 tablespoons shelled, roasted pistachios
- 2 tablespoons balsamic vinegar or white balsamic vinegar
- 2 teaspoons honey
- 12 fresh basil leaves, roughly chopped
- 2 sprigs of fresh thyme, chopped
- 1 garlic clove, grated
- Crushed red pepper flakes
- Kosher salt
- 2½ cups cherry tomatoes halved
- 2 nectarines, cut into wedges
- 2 balls of burrata cheese, roughly torn
- 2 tablespoons chopped fresh chives, for serving
- Flaky sea salt, for serving

INSTRUCTIONS:
a) In a food processor, combine the olive oil, pistachios, vinegar, honey, basil, thyme, garlic, red pepper flakes, and a pinch of salt and pulse until finely ground, about 1 minute.

b) In a medium bowl, combine the tomatoes and nectarines. Add the pistachio puree, tossing to coat. Let marinate at room temperature for 10 to 20 minutes or covered with plastic wrap overnight in the fridge.

c) To serve, divide the salad evenly among six bowls and top each with some torn burrata, chives, and a pinch of flaky salt.

45. Pistachio salad

Makes: 8 servings

INGREDIENTS:
- 9 ounces pk. whipped topping
- 1 pack pistachio pudding
- 1 can crushed pineapple, drained
- 1 cup miniature marshmallows

INSTRUCTIONS:
a) Fold dry pudding mix into whipped topping. add pineapple and marshmallows.
b) Refrigerate until firm.

46. Almond pistachio saffron curry sauce

Makes: 2 Servings

INGREDIENTS:
- ½ cup Raw unblanched almonds
- ½ cup Shelled; unsalted raw pistachio nuts
- 2 tablespoons Butter or mild vegetable oil
- 1 large Onion; peeled and grated
- ½ teaspoon Ground coriander
- ¼ teaspoon Mace
- ½ teaspoon Freshly ground white pepper
- 2 Green cardamom pods; husked, ground
- ½ teaspoon Cayenne pepper
- 1 pinch Nutmeg
- ½ teaspoon Saffron threads, soaked in 2 tablespoons hot water
- 2 cups Heavy cream
- ¾ teaspoon Salt; or to taste

INSTRUCTIONS:
a) Combine almonds and pistachios in a 10-inch frying pan and dry-roast over medium heat for 8 to 10 minutes. Place in a blender or a food processor and reduce to a powder. Set aside.

b) Heat butter in a heavy 2-quart saucepan over medium-high heat.

c) Add onion and cook until lightly browned. Stir in spices and cook until fragrant, about 1 minute. Stir in saffron, cream, salt, and powdered nuts. Bring to a boil, stirring constantly.

d) Reduce heat and simmer, stirring occasionally, until sauce is thick enough to coat the back of a spoon, 12 to 15 minutes.

47. Pistachio soup

Makes: 4

INGREDIENTS:
- 2 tbsp boiling water
- ¼ tsp saffron threads
- 1⅔ cups / 200 g shelled unsalted pistachios
- 2 tbsp / 30 g unsalted butter
- 4 shallots, finely chopped (3½ oz / 100 g in total)
- 1 oz / 25 g ginger, peeled and finely chopped
- 1 leek, finely chopped (1¼ cups / 150 g in total)
- 2 tsp ground cumin
- 3 cups / 700 ml chicken stock
- ⅓ cup / 80 ml freshly squeezed orange juice
- 1 tbsp freshly squeezed lemon juice
- salt and freshly ground black pepper
- sour cream, to serve

a) Preheat the oven to 350°F / 180°C. Pour the boiling water over the saffron threads in a small cup and leave to infuse for 30 minutes.

b) To remove the pistachio skins, blanch the nuts in boiling water for 1 minute, drain, and while still hot, remove the skins by pressing the nuts between your fingers. Not all the skins will come off as with almonds—this is fine as it won't affect the soup—but getting rid of some skin will improve the color, making it a brighter green. Spread the pistachios out on a baking sheet and roast in the oven for 8 minutes. Remove and leave to cool.

c) Heat the butter in a large saucepan and add the shallots, ginger, leek, cumin, ½ teaspoon salt, and some black pepper. Sauté over medium heat for 10 minutes, stirring often, until the shallots are completely soft. Add the stock and half of the saffron liquid. Cover the pan, lower the heat, and let the soup simmer for 20 minutes.

d) Place all but 1 tablespoon of the pistachios in a large bowl along with half of the soup. Use a handheld blender to blitz until smooth and then return this to the saucepan. Add the orange and lemon juice, reheat, and taste to adjust the seasoning.

e) To serve, coarsely chop up the reserved pistachios. Transfer the hot soup into bowls and top with a spoonful of sour cream. Sprinkle with the pistachios and drizzle with the remaining saffron liquid.

48. Avocado-Pistachio Pesto Noodle Salad

Makes: 4 SERVINGS

INGREDIENTS:
- 1 (12-ounce) package kelp noodles
- 4 cups herbed spring salad mixture, lightly packed
- 1 recipe Avocado-Pistachio Pesto

a) Place all the ingredients in a mixing bowl and toss everything together well.

49. Chicory & Citrus Salad with Shaved Fennel

Makes: 6 to 8

INGREDIENTS:
- 2 tablespoons red wine vinegar
- Kosher salt and freshly ground black pepper
- 3 tablespoons extra virgin olive oil, plus more for drizzling
- 1 small red onion, halved and thinly sliced
- 2 navel oranges
- Flaky sea salt
- 1 cup thinly sliced fennel bulb (about ½ bulb)
- ½ pound mixed chicories (such as red or Castelfranco radicchio, or frisée), trimmed, leaves separated and torn into large pieces
- ½ loosely packed cup fresh flat-leaf parsley leaves
- ¼ cup roasted unsalted pistachios, chopped

a) Marinate the onion. Place the vinegar in a large bowl. Whisk in 1 teaspoon kosher salt and ¼ teaspoon pepper. Slowly whisk in the tablespoons olive oil. Add the onion and toss to combine.
b) Set aside for 10 minutes to marinate.
c) Prepare the oranges. Cut a small section off the top and bottom of the oranges so they can stand flat.
d) Use a sharp knife to cut away the peel (including the pith) and then cut the oranges crosswise into ¼-inch-thick rounds.
e) Arrange the orange slices on a large serving plate. Season with flaky salt.
f) Finish and serve the salad. Add the fennel, chicories, parsley, and pistachios to the bowl of onion. Lightly drizzle with olive oil and season with salt and pepper. Toss to combine.
g) Arrange the salad on top of the orange slices and serve.

DESSERT

50. Apricot and pistachio soufflé

Makes: 6 - 8

INGREDIENTS:
- 3 tablespoons Butter
- 4 tablespoons Flour
- 1½ cup Milk
- 6 Egg yolks
- 8 Egg whites
- pinch Salt
- ⅛ teaspoon Cream of tartar
- ½ Apricot and Pineapple Jam
- ½ Apricot and Pineapple Jam
- ¼ teaspoon Almond extract
- 2 Almond extract
- whipped cream
- dried apricots, soaked
- shelled pistachio nuts
- apricot brandy
- confectioners' sugar
- Ground pistachio nuts

INSTRUCTIONS:
a) Preheat oven to 400-F.
b) Melt the butter and add the flour. Add the milk gradually stirring with a wire whisk to make a thick smooth sauce.
c) Add the sugar. Remove from the heat and add the egg yolks one at a time.
d) Add the almond extract, the drained, chopped apricots, the pistachio nuts, and the optional brandy. Beat the egg whites, with a pinch of salt and the cream of tartar, until stiff.
e) Fold in apricot mixture and spoon into a buttered and sugared 6 cup soufflé dish. Place the soufflé in the oven and immediately reduce the heat to 375 F. Bake for 25 minutes.

51. Pistachio soufflé with pistachio ice cream

Makes: 6

INGREDIENTS:
FOR THE ICE CREAM
- 4 large eggs, separated
- 100g golden caster sugar
- 300ml double cream
- 2 tablespoons pistachio paste

FOR THE SOUFFLÉ
- melted butter, for the dishes
- 3 tablespoons caster sugar, plus extra for the dishes
- 3 large eggs, separated
- 1 tablespoon corn flour
- 1 tablespoon plain flour
- 250ml whole milk
- 2 tablespoons pistachio paste

INSTRUCTIONS:
a) Make the ice cream the day before. Whisk the egg whites to stiff peaks using electric beaters, then gradually beat in the sugar, whisking after each addition until you have a smooth, glossy meringue.

b) Using the same beaters whisk the cream with the pistachio paste to soft peaks.

c) Fold the cream and egg yolks through the meringue, spoon into a container, and freeze for six hours, or overnight.

d) To make the soufflés, brush the inside of six ramekins with melted butter, then coat them with caster sugar.

e) Whisk the egg yolks with 2 tablespoons of sugar, the flour, and a pinch of salt. Heat the milk with the pistachio paste until just steaming then, whisking constantly, pour the liquid onto the egg yolk mixture.

f) Clean out the milk pan, then pour the mixture back in, return to the heat, and cook for 2-3 mins until it's the consistency of thick custard. Remove from the heat and cover the surface with cling film until needed.

g) When ready to eat, heat the oven to 200C and put a baking sheet on the top shelf to heat up.

h) Using electric beaters, whisk the egg whites to medium-stiff peaks, then whisk in the remaining sugar.

i) Mix a large spoonful of the egg whites into the pistachio mixture, then carefully fold in the rest.

j) Divide between the ramekins, then run a cutlery knife around the top edge of each of the ramekins.

k) Transfer to the hot baking sheet and cook for 8-12 mins until well risen.

l) Serve straight away topped with pistachio ice cream.

52. Pistachio Matcha Ice Cream

Makes: 8 small ice creams

INGREDIENTS:
- 2 teaspoons Green Tea matcha powder
- ½ cup pistachios shelled
- ½ cup cashews
- ½ cup coconut milk
- 1 cup coconut flesh
- 2 teaspoons vanilla bean paste
- ¼ cup maple syrup
- 3 tablespoons coconut oil melted
- 100g good quality dark chocolate or raw chocolate, melted

INSTRUCTIONS:
a)   Mix pistachios and cashews in a food processor or high-powered blender and blitz to a fine crumb.

b)   Add coconut milk, coconut flesh, vanilla, Green Tea matcha powder, and maple, and blitz until smooth.

c)   Keep the blender running whilst pouring in melted coconut oil. This should create a beautiful creamy consistency in the blend.

d)   Pour into ice cream molds or ramekins and freeze for 2-3 hours to set.

e)   To serve, remove ice creams from molds, place them on a tray lined with baking paper, and drizzle over molten chocolate.

f)   Place back in the fridge to set for a minute or two and then serve.

53. Pomegranate possets with pistachio biscotti

Makes: 4-6

INGREDIENTS:
FOR THE POSSET
- 180ml pomegranate juice
- 600ml double cream
- 135g caster sugar
- Zest of ½ lemon

FOR THE BISCOTTI
- 250g plain flour
- 1 tablespoon baking powder
- 250g caster sugar
- 110g pistachios
- Zest of ½ lemon
- 2 eggs
- 1 egg yolk

TO SERVE
- 50g pomegranate seeds
- Zest of 1 lemon

INSTRUCTIONS:
a) To make the posset, put all the ingredients in a medium-sized pan. Bring to a boil while stirring with a whisk, then turn the heat down slightly and simmer for 4 minutes.

b) Pour the mix through a fine sieve, skim with a spoon or ladle to ensure your possets have a smooth clean finish, then pour into your choice of serving glasses.

c) For the biscotti, mix the flour, baking powder, sugar, pistachios, and lemon zest. In another bowl, beat the eggs and egg yolk together.

d) Add the egg to the dry ingredients gradually, mixing constantly until the dough comes together. Roll out into an oval 3cm deep and chill in the fridge for one hour. Meanwhile, preheat the oven to 180C/350F/gas mark 4.

e) Remove from the fridge and put on a baking tray lined with baking parchment. Put in the oven for 20 minutes then leave to cool.

f) Once cool, cut into 1cm-thick slices, at an angle. Return the slices to the baking tray, turn the oven down to 140C/275F/gas mark 1 and bake for 6-10 minutes, until the slices are set in the middle. Remove and place on a cooling rack.

g) To serve, put the fresh pomegranate seeds on top of the posset, with the grated lemon zest and the biscotti on the side.

54. Goji, Pistachio, and Lemon Tart

Makes: 12

INGREDIENTS:
FOR THE RAW VEGAN PISTACHIO CRUST:
- 1½ cup almond flour or almond meal
- ½ cup pistachios
- 3 dates
- 1½ tablespoon coconut oil
- ½ teaspoon ground cardamom powder
- ⅛ teaspoon salt

FILLING:
- 1½ cups coconut cream
- 1 cup lemon juice
- 1 tablespoon cornstarch
- 2 teaspoon agar-agar
- ¼ cup maple syrup
- ½ teaspoon ground turmeric powder
- 1 teaspoon vanilla extract
- ½ teaspoon goji extract

TOPPINGS:
- a handful of goji berries
- dragon fruit
- edible flowers
- chocolate hearts

INSTRUCTIONS:
TART SHELL
a) Blend the almond flour and pistachios in a food processor/blender till a fine crumb.
b) Add the rest of the crust **INGREDIENTS:** and mix well until you obtain a uniform sticky mixture.
c) Add the crust dough to a tart tin and spread it evenly within the base.
d) Leave to chill in the fridge, while you prepare the filling.
FILLING

e) Heat the coconut cream in a medium saucepan, stirring well till smooth and uniform.

f) Add the rest of the filling **INGREDIENTS:**, including the cornstarch and agar agar.

g) While stirring continuously, bring to a boil and cook for a few minutes until it begins to thicken.

h) When the mixture thickens, remove it from the heat and leave it to cool down for 10-15 minutes.

i) Then pour over the crust and leave it to cool completely.

j) Place in the fridge for a couple of hours at least, till the filling is completely set.

k) Decorate with goji berries, dragon fruit balls, and edible flowers, or with your favorite toppings.

55. Vanilla Pistachio Ice Cream

Makes: 4

INGREDIENTS:
- 2 cups pistachios
- 1 ½ cups water
- ½ cup virgin coconut oil
- ¼ cup packed Sea Moss
- ½ cup coconut nectar
- ¼ teaspoons vanilla powder
- 2 teaspoons vanilla extract
- ¼ teaspoons mineral salt
- Date paste to taste

INSTRUCTIONS:
a) Blend the nuts with water to make a thick cream. Strain the mixture through a nut milk bag.
b) Blend 1 cup of pistachio milk with the Sea Moss until very smooth.
c) Add the remainder of the ingredients and blend until smooth.
d) Pour into a freezable container and let freeze overnight.

56. Lemon meringue–pistachio pie

Makes: 10-Inch Pie

INGREDIENTS:
- 1 serving Pistachio Crunch
- ½ ounce white chocolate, melted
- 1⅓ cups Lemon Curd
- 1 cup sugar
- ½ cup water
- 3 egg whites
-]¼ cup Lemon Curd

INSTRUCTIONS:
a) Dump the pistachio crunch into a 10-inch pie tin. With your fingers and the palms of your hands, press the crunch firmly into the pie tin, making sure the bottom and sides are evenly covered. Set aside while you make the filling; wrapped in plastic, the crust can be refrigerated, for up to 2 weeks.

b) Using a pastry brush, paint a thin layer of the white chocolate onto the bottom and up the sides of the crust. Put the crust in the freezer for 10 minutes to set the chocolate.

c) Put 1⅓ cups lemon curd into a small bowl and stir to loosen it a bit. Scrape the lemon curd into a crust and use the back of a spoon or a spatula to spread it in an even layer. Place the pie in the freezer for about 10 minutes to help set the lemon curd layer.

d) Meanwhile, combine the sugar and water in a small heavy-bottomed saucepan and gently slush the sugar around in the water until it feels like wet sand. Place the saucepan over medium heat and heat the mixture up to 239°F, keeping track of the temperature with an instant-read or candy thermometer.

e) While the sugar is heating up, put the egg whites in the bowl of a stand mixer and, with the whisk attachment, begin whipping them to medium-soft peaks.

f) Once the sugar syrup reaches 239°F, remove it from the heat and very carefully pour it into the whipping egg whites, being sure to avoid the whisk: turn the mixer down to very low speed before you do this, unless you want some interesting burn marks on your face.

g) Once all of the sugar is successfully added to the egg whites, turn the mixer speed back up and let the meringue whip until it has cooled to room temperature.

h) While the meringue is whipping, put the ¼ cup lemon curd in a large bowl and stir, using a spatula, to loosen it up a bit.

i) When the meringue has cooled to room temperature, turn the mixer off, remove the bowl, and fold the meringue into the lemon curd with the spatula until no white streaks remain, being careful not to deflate the meringue.

j) Remove the pie from the freezer and scoop the lemon meringue on top of the lemon curd. Using a spoon, spread the meringue in an even layer, completely covering the lemon curd.

k) Serve, or store the pie in the freezer until ready to use. Wrapped tightly in plastic wrap once frozen hard, it will keep in the freezer for up to 3 weeks. Let the pie defrost overnight in the fridge or for at least 3 hours at room temperature before serving.

57. Pistachio layer cake

Makes: 6-Inch Layer Cake

INGREDIENTS:
- 1 serving Pistachio Cake
- 65 g pistachio oil [⅓ cup]
- 1 serving Lemon Curd
- ½ serving Milk Crumb
- 1 serving Pistachio Frosting

INSTRUCTIONS:
a) Put a piece of parchment or a Silpat on the counter. Invert the cake onto it and peel off the parchment or Silpat from the bottom of the cake. Use the cake ring to stamp out 2 circles from the cake. These are your top 2 cake layers. The remaining cake "scrap" will come together to make the bottom layer of the cake.

LAYER 1, THE BOTTOM
b) Clean the cake ring and place it in the center of a sheet pan lined with clean parchment or a Silpat. Use 1 strip of acetate to line the inside of the cake ring.

c) Put the cake scraps inside the ring and use the back of your hand to tamp the scraps together into a flat even layer.

d) Dunk a pastry brush in the pistachio oil and give the layer of cake a good, healthy bath of half of the oil.

e) Use the back of a spoon to spread half of the lemon curd in an even layer over the cake.

f) Sprinkle one-third of the milk crumbs evenly over the lemon curd. Use the back of your hand to anchor them in place.

g) Use the back of a spoon to spread one-third of the pistachio frosting as evenly as possible over the crumbs.

LAYER 2, THE MIDDLE
h) With your index finger, gently tuck the second strip of acetate between the cake ring and the top ¼ inch of the first strip of acetate, so that you have a clear ring of acetate 5 to 6 inches tall—high enough to support the height of the finished cake. Set a cake round on top of the frosting, and repeat the process for layer 1.

LAYER 3, THE TOP

i) Nestle the remaining cake round into the frosting. Cover the top of the cake with the remaining frosting. Give it volume and swirls, or do as we do and opt for a perfectly flat top. Garnish the frosting with the remaining milk crumbs.

j) Transfer the sheet pan to the freezer and freeze for a minimum of 12 hours to set the cake and filling. The cake will keep in the freezer for up to 2 weeks.

k) At least 3 hours before you are ready to serve the cake, pull the sheet pan out of the freezer and, using your fingers and thumbs, pop the cake out of the cake ring. Gently peel off the acetate, and transfer the cake to a platter or cake stand. Let it defrost in the fridge for a minimum of 3 hours.

58. Pistachio cake

Makes: 1 Quarter Sheet Pan Cake

INGREDIENTS:
- ¼ cup pistachio paste
- 3 tablespoons glucose
- 6 egg whites
- 1¾ cups confectioners' sugar
- 1¼ cups blanched almond flour
- ½ cup pistachio oil
- ¼ cup heavy cream
- 1 cup flour
- 1½ teaspoons baking powder
- 1½ teaspoons kosher salt

INSTRUCTIONS:
a) Heat the oven to 350°F.

b) Combine the pistachio paste and glucose in the bowl of a stand mixer fitted with the paddle attachment and beat on medium-low for 2 to 3 minutes, until the mixture turns into a sticky green paste. Scrape down the sides of the bowl with a spatula.

c) On low speed, add the egg whites one at a time, being careful not to add the next egg white until the previous one is completely incorporated. Stop the mixer and scrape down the sides of the bowl with a spatula after every 2 to 3 egg whites. Once all of the egg whites have been incorporated, you will have a snotty green soup in your mixing bowl. Right on.

d) Add the confectioners' sugar and almond flour and, on low speed, paddle them in for 2 to 3 minutes, until the mixture thickens. Stop the mixer and scrape down the sides of the bowl.

e) Stream in the pistachio oil and heavy cream and paddle on low speed for 1 minute. Stop the mixer and scrape down the sides of the bowl.

f) Add the flour, baking powder, and salt and paddle on low for 2 to 3 minutes, until the batter is super-smooth and slightly more viscous than your average American box cake batter.

g) Pam-spray a quarter sheet pan and line it with parchment, or just line the pan with a Silpat. Using a spatula, spread the cake batter in an even layer in the pan. Bake for 20 to 22 minutes. The cake will rise and puff, doubling in size.

h) At 20 minutes, gently poke the edge of the cake with your finger: the cake should bounce back, and it should be slightly golden brown on the sides and pulling away from the sides of the pan ever so slightly. Leave the cake in the oven for an extra 1 to 2 minutes if it doesn't pass these tests.

i) Take the cake out of the oven and cool on a wire rack.

j)

59. Pistachio Kulfi

Makes: 6 servings

INGREDIENTS:
- 6 oz pistachio nuts
- 284ml carton double cream
- ½ pint full cream milk
- 1 tbsp caster sugar
- ¼ tsp ground cardamom
- ½ tsp vanilla extract

INSTRUCTIONS:
a) Put the pistachio nuts into a food processor or blender and buzz until very finely chopped.

b) Tip the ground nuts into a large saucepan and stir in the cream, milk, sugar and cardamom.

c) Bring slowly to the boil, stirring, then bubble gently for 3–5 minutes until thickened, stirring all the time to prevent the mixture catching on the bottom of the pan.

d) Remove from the heat and stir in the vanilla. Leave to cool.

e) Cover and refrigerate for about 30 minutes or until well chilled.

f) Tip the mixture into the ice cream machine and freeze according to instructions.

g) Transfer to a suitable container or into individual moulds and freeze until required.

h) Serve sprinkled with the remaining pistachio nuts.

60. Nutty Pistachio Ice Cream

Makes: 1 1/4 quarts

INGREDIENTS:
- 1 cup half–and–half
- 3/4 cup granulated sugar
- 1/8 teaspoon salt
- 2 egg yolks, beaten
- 1 tablespoon vanilla extract
- 2 cups heavy cream
- 1 cup blanched, natural California pistachios, chopped
- 1 tablespoon finely grated orange peel

INSTRUCTIONS:
a) Heat half–and–half in saucepan; stir in sugar and salt. Pour a small amount of hot half–and–half into egg yolks, stirring constantly. Return yolk mixture to half–and–half; cook and stir over medium heat about 5 to 10 minutes or until thickened and creamy. Do not boil. Cool.

b) Stir in vanilla extract and heavy cream. Chill.

c) Pour into freezer container; follow manufacturer's **INSTRUCTIONS:** for freezing. Add pistachios and orange peel when almost frozen; freeze until firm.

d) Allow ice cream to stand at least 2 hours in refrigerator–freezer to mellow flavors.

e) Drop shelled nuts into boiling water, remove from heat and let them soak for about one minute.

f) Drain and rub the pistachios with a clean kitchen towel.

g) To dry, spread on a large baking sheet in an oven preheated to 300 degrees F for 10 to 15 minutes.

61. Pistachio pudding

Makes: 6 servings

INGREDIENTS:
- 1 pack Instant pistachio
- Pudding mix
- 1 large Can crushed pineapple
- 1 cup Miniature marshmallows
- 1 large Cool whip
- ½ cup Nuts

INSTRUCTIONS:
a) Mix all ingredients and refrigerate for 2 hours or overnight.
b) Decorate with maraschino cherries if desired.
c) Keeps well if covered in refrigerator.

62. Strawberry pistachio mille-feuillantines

Makes: 20 wafers

INGREDIENTS:
WAFERS
- ½ cup Shelled natural pistachios
- ¼ cup All-purpose flour
- ½ cup Granulated sugar
- ¼ teaspoon Salt
- 2 larges Egg whites
- 5 tablespoons Unsalted butter, melted
- ¼ teaspoon Vanilla

WHIPPED CREAM
- 1 vanilla bean, cut lengthwise
- 1 cup Chilled heavy cream
- 3 tablespoons Granulated sugar

TO SERVE
- 1 pounds Small strawberries
- Confectioners' sugar for dusting
- 4 smalls Strawberries and chopped pistachios

INSTRUCTIONS:
MAKE WAFERS:
a) Preheat oven to 325° F. and spray a heavy or non-stick baking sheet with cooking spray or line with parchment paper.

b) Rub off loose skins from pistachios and in a food processor grind nuts with granulated sugar.

c) In a bowl whisk together pistachio mixture, flour, and salt and whisk in whites, butter, and vanilla until combined well.

d) Drop rounded teaspoons batter 5 inches apart onto baking sheet and with back of a spoon spread into 3½- to 4-inch rounds.

e) Bake wafers in middle of oven Working quickly, transfer hot wafers with a thin metal spatula to a rack to cool completely.

f) Make more wafers with remaining batter in same manner, spraying or re-lining sheet for each batch.

MAKE WHIPPED CREAM

g) Into a chilled bowl scrape seeds of vanilla bean and add cream and granulated sugar.

h) With a whisk or an electric mixer beat mixture until it holds stiff peaks.

TO ASSEMBLE

i) Put a wafer in center of each of 4 plates.

j) Spread about 2 tablespoons whipped cream on each wafer, leaving a ¼-inch border, and top with half of strawberries.

k) Put another wafer on top of strawberries and top in same manner with remaining cream and strawberries.

l) Dust 4 wafers with confectioners' sugar and put on top of desserts.

m) Garnish each mille-feuillantine with a strawberry and sprinkle plates with pistachios.

63. Blackberry Honey Panna Cotta

Makes: 6

INGREDIENTS:
- 1 cup kefir or buttermilk
- 4oz envelope unflavored, powdered gelatin
- 2 cups heavy cream
- 1 vanilla bean, split
- 1/4 cup Blackberry Honey
- 1/4 teaspoon kosher salt
- Handful pistachios, chopped

INSTRUCTIONS
a) Measure the kefir and sprinkle the gelatin evenly over the top, but do not stir. Let the gelatin soften until the grains look wet and like they are beginning to dissolve, 5-10 minutes.

b) Meanwhile, heat the cream, honey, salt and vanilla bean in a saucepan set over medium heat until just barely simmering. Stir occasionally to dissolve the honey. Turn off the heat and remove the vanilla bean, scraping the seeds into the pot.

c) Add the milk and gelatin and stir until the gelatin dissolves. Divide the mixture between 6 ramekins or glasses. Cover and chill until set, at least 4 hours and up to overnight. If you are going to leave them overnight, cover each ramekin with plastic wrap.

d) To unmold the panna cottas, run a thin knife around the top edge of each ramekin to release the sides, and invert it onto a plate. You may have to shake the ramekin gently to get the panna cotta to release onto the plate. Top each panna cotta with a spoonful pf rhubarb and it's juices and sprinkle of chopped pistachios.

e) Alternately, serve the panna cottas straight from their ramekins with the garnishes on top.

64. Creme Fraiche Panna Cotta with blackberries

Makes: 6

INGREDIENTS:
- 1 cup whole milk
- 1 cup heavy cream
- ½ cup granulated sugar
- ⅔ cup crème fraiche
- 4 sheets gelatin or 1 tablespoon powdered gelatin
- garnish
- fresh blackberries
- crushed pistachios
- white chocolate crispy balls, optional

INSTRUCTIONS

a) Pour milk, cream, sugar, and crème fraiche into a saucepan and whisk until smooth.

b) Place saucepan over medium-low to medium heat and simmer until sugar dissolves, stirring.

c) Fill a mixing bowl with ice water and add gelatin sheets to "bloom". Once sheets have become soft and pliable, stir them into the milk mixture.

d) Stir until gelatin dissolves.

e) Remove milk mixture from the stove and pour into 6 4-ounce ramekins. Transfer filled ramekins to a baking sheet and place in the refrigerator to set. Allow panna cottas to set up in the refrigerator for at least 4 to 6 hours and up to 2 days.

f) Top with berries, pistachios and white chocolate crispy balls, if using. Serve.

65. Buttermilk Goat Cheese Panna Cotta with Figs

Makes: 6-8 servings

INGREDIENTS:
PANNA COTTA:
- 2 cups heavy cream
- 2/3 cup sugar
- ¼ tsp kosher salt
- 1 cup buttermilk
- 2 tsp plain powdered gelatin
- ¼ tsp finely grated orange zest
- 4 oz creamy, fresh goat cheese, softened at room temperature

NUTS:
- ½ cup pistachios
- 2 tsp unsalted butter, melted
- Kosher salt

OTHER TOPPINGS:
- Orange blossom honey
- Fresh figs, cut into wedges

INSTRUCTIONS
a) Heat cream base: Add cream, sugar and salt to a pot. Bring to a simmer over medium heat, stirring occasionally.

b) Bloom gelatin: Place buttermilk in a cup. Sprinkle gelatin over top. Allow to bloom for 5-10 minutes while cream comes to a simmer.

c) Mix panna cotta base: When cream comes to a simmer, lower heat and whisk in buttermilk/gelatin mixture. Stir in orange zest. Whisk until gelatin is dissolved. Place softened goat cheese in a bowl. Whisk cream mixture into goat cheese, one ladleful at a time, until completely combined.

d) Strain and pour: Strain panna cotta base through a sieve into a large liquid measuring cup. Pour mixture into desired glasses or ramekins. This is enough for 6-8 servings. Cool at room temperature. Place in fridge to cool and set up completely for several hours or ideally overnight.

e) Toast pistachios: While panna cotta sets up, toast the pistachios. Preheat oven to 350°F. Place nuts on a parchment lined baking sheet. Drizzle over melted butter and season liberally with salt. Toss. Bake about 8-10 minutes or until golden brown. Cool at room temperature and store in an airtight container.

f) Serve: To serve, top panna cottas with figs and nuts, and drizzle over honey. Enjoy.

66. Pistachio Panna Cotta

Makes: 4

INGREDIENTS:
- 1 can coconut milk 400 mls
- 3 tbsp sugar
- 3/4 tsp agar-agar
- 1 tbsp cold water
- 1/4 cup Pistacho butter
- 1/2 tsp orange blossom water

INSTRUCTIONS

a) In a small bowl, place the tablespoon of cold water, then sprinkle the agar-agar in a layer over top. Allow it to sit for a few minutes while you complete the next step.

b) In a medium saucepan, place the coconut milk, sugar and pistacho butter. Whisk together and heat until everything is melted together and steaming, but don't allow to boil.

c) Pour a couple of tablespoons of the hot coconut milk into the bowl with the agar-agar, and stir well. Add it slowly back into the pot, whisking the whole time. Heat for another 5 minutes, until the milk is steaming, but don't let it boil. Whisk in the orange flower water at the end.

d) Divide between 4 ramekins. Refrigerate until set.

e) To unmold, remove from the fridge and place the ramekin in a hot water bath for a few minutes. Run an offset spatula or a butter knife around the edges of the panna cotta. Place a plate on top of the panna cotta and invert. It should slide out onto the plate. Garnish with flower petals and additional pistachios.

67. Roasted Rhubarb and Pistachio Panna Cotta

INGREDIENTS:
- 1/2 pound thin rhubarb stalks
- 1/2 cup granulated sugar
- juice of 1/2 lemon
- 1 vanilla bean, split
- 1/2 cup chopped pistachios, to serve

INSTRUCTIONS

a) Heat oven to 375ºF.

b) Slice the rhubarb into 2-3 inch lengths. Toss it in a baking dish with the sugar, lemon juice and vanilla bean. Roast until soft and juicy but not falling apart, about 15-20 minutes.

c) Let cool before serving.

68. Cardamom and Blood Orange Panna Cotta

INGREDIENTS:
BLOOD ORANGE AND CARDAMOM PANNA COTTA:
- 1 1/2 cup almond milk
- 1/2 cup coconut cream
- 1/2 cup freshly squeezed blood orange juice
- 1 envelop gelatin
- 1/4 cup organic cane sugar
- 2 tbsp honey
- 1 tsp cardamom powder
- 1 tsp vanilla bean paste or 1 tsp vanilla bean extract

BLOOD ORANGE JELLY:
- 1 1/2 cups + 1/2 cup blood orange juice, divided
- 2 envelops of gelatin
- 1 tsp of blood orange zest
- 1/3 cup organic cane sugar
- 1/4 tsp salt

TOASTED QUINOA CRUMBLE:
- 1/2 cup quinoa
- 3 tbsp maple syrup or honey
- 1 tbsp coconut oil
- 1/4 tsp salt
- 1/4 tsp cardamom powder
- 2 tbsp freeze dried raspberries
- 2 tbsp toasted pistachios coarsely chopped

GARNISH:
- 2 blood orange slices cut into half

INSTRUCTIONS
BLOOD ORANGE AND CARDAMOM PANNA COTTA:
a) In a small saucepan, sprinkle gelatin over 1 cup room temperature almond milk. Let stand for 1 minute to soften. Heat the gelatin mixture over low heat until gelatin is dissolved and remove pan from heat.

b) In a large saucepan, bring remaining almond milk, coconut cream, blood orange juice, honey, sugar, cardamom powder, salt, vanilla bean extract together and stir to bring to just a boil over moderate heat. Remove pan from heat after the boil and stir in gelatin mixture. Let it cool.

c) Divide the mixture equally into 4 wine glasses and let it sit in the fridge for 4 hours or overnight.

BLOOD ORANGE JELLY:

d) Warm up 1 1/2 cups of the blood orange juice. Mix the 2 gelatin envelops with 1/2 cup of the blood orange juice and mix with the warm juice. Add in the sugar and zest and whisk until combined and sugar is dissolved.

e) Pour it gently and equally into the 4 glasses and let it set in the fridge.

TOASTED QUINOA CRUMBLE:

f) Preheat oven to 350 degrees.

g) In a small bowl, toss all the ingredients except the raspberries, and gently spread it on a small baking pan. Bake in the oven for about 20 minutes. Let it cool. Break it apart into crumbles.

ASSEMBLY:

h) Put about 1-2 tsp of the toasted quinoa crumble into each glass. Crumble some freeze dried raspberries on the top, along with some chopped pistachios.

i) Add half a slice of the blood orange on top of each panna cotta assembled neatly. The panna cottas are ready to be served and eaten!

69. Cardamom-honey Yoghurt Panna cotta

INGREDIENTS:
3 tbsp gelatin powder
500 ml milk
100 gm caster sugar
1 1/2 tbsp cardamom powder
200 gm yoghurt
3 tbsp honey+ extra honey to serve
2 tbsp unsalted butter
1 drop vanilla essence
1/2 ripe mango cut into small diced pieces for garnish

INSTRUCTIONS:
a) Heat the milk, sugar, cardamom powder in a pot until the sugar has dissolved. Bring to boil, then add 3 tbsp gelatin powder and boil this milk.stirring continuously for 3-4 minutes or till it is completely dissolved.

b) Remove from heat and add 1 drop vanilla essence and mix it well. And leave to cool for 15 minutes.
c) After 15 minutes whisk the yoghurt honey and 1/2 tsp cardamom powder in a bowl. Pour into the mil and slowly whisk and mix it well.
d) Rinse pudding mould or bowl with cold water, the divide the mixture between them while the mould or bowl are still wet. Chill in the refrigerator for 3-4 hours or overnight until set.
e) When ready to serve, loosen the edge of each yoghurt with knife, ten dip the base into arm water for 5 sec. Turn out onto serving plate.
f) Garnish with the pistachio and diced mango and drizzle ove a little extra honey to serve.

70. Pistachio and Basil Panna Cotta

4 servings

INGREDIENTS:
1 cup heavy cream
1/4 cup fresh basil, chopped
1/4 cup blanched and pureed pistachios
1/2 cup sugar
3/4 cup milk
3 tsp powdered gelatin
2-3 drops pistachio essence (optional)
INSTRUCTIONS:

Combine cream, basil, pistachio puree and sugar, in a saucepan and put it on the heat.

First, bring to a boil and then let it simmer for 5 mins. Remove from heat and let the mixture steep for 15 minutes.

Pour through a fine-mash sieve or muslin cloth, into a bowl to remove solids.

In another saucepan, pour 1/2 cup milk and let it heat. Remove from heat, add powdered gelatin and let it sit for a couple of mins. Put it back on heat and let the milk simmer for 2 mins.

Mix the gelatin and milk mixture with the cream mixture prepared before and stir well.

Lightly grease the moulds in which you'the like to set your pannacotta.

Pour the mixture in the moulds and refrigerate until chilled and set. This will take about 3-4 hours.

Unmould on the plate or have it in the mould itself. Garnish with chopped pistachios or with your favourite fresh berries or compote.

71. Saffron Pistachio Panna Cotta

Makes: 2 servings

INGREDIENTS:
- 2 tablespoon Soft paneer or homemade cottage cheese
- 2 teaspoon Sugar
- 2 tablespoon Milk
- 1 tablespoon Cream
- 1 pinch Saffron
- 1 big pinch Agar agar powder
- 2 teaspoon Pistachio
- 1 pinch Cardamom powder

INSTRUCTIONS:
Mash soft paneer and sugar powder till smooth.
Boil 2 tablespoon milk &1 tablespoon cream and a pinch of Saffron together.
Add a big pinch of agag agar powder.
Whisk till smooth.
Add paneer mix, cardamom powder and chopped pistachio. Mix well.
In a greased mould add 1/4 teaspoon chopped pistachio. Pour panna cotta mix.
Chill for 2 hours in refrigerator.
Unmould and serve. Add some syrup of your choice and fruits on top.
You can adjust sugar as per taste.

72. Rose yogurt panna cotta

Makes: 2 servings

INGREDIENTS:
- 1/2 cup fresh cream
- 1/2 cup yogurt
- 1 tbsp sugar
- 3 tbsp rose syrup
- 1/4 tsp rose colour
- 1.5 tsp agar agar
- 1 tbsp water
- Few Drops Rose Essence
- Pistachios

INSTRUCTIONS:
a) In a large bowl mix yogurt, 1 tbsp cream, Rose syrup and Rose essence, whisk until well combined and smooth.

b) In a small bowl whisk Agar powder into warm water until combined.

c) In a small pan or saucepan heat remaining cream and sugar over low to medium flame, stirring often. Once sugar is dissolved add agar powder mixture and continue stirring until mixture is hot and simmering but not boiling. It will take around 1-2 minutes. Make sure not to boil this mixture.

d) Now pour this mixture into yogurt mixture and whisk until well combined. You will need to do this faster as agar will start to set.

e) Divide this Panna cotta mixture in greased or silicone bowls and chill into refrigerator until set or at least for 4 hours.

f) De-mould Rose Yogurt Panna Cotta from the ramekins and serve with chopped pistachios on the top.

73. No-Bake Choc Chip Cannoli Cheesecake

Makes: 8 servings

INGREDIENTS:
- 4 ounces cannoli shells
- ½ cup sugar
- ½ cup graham cracker crumbs
- ⅓ cup butter, melted

FILLING:
- Two 8 ounces packages of cream cheese, softened
- 1 cup confectioners' sugar
- ½ teaspoon grated orange zest
- ¼ teaspoon ground cinnamon
- ¾ cup part-skim ricotta cheese
- 1 teaspoon vanilla extract
- ½ teaspoon rum extract
- ½ cup miniature semisweet chocolate chips
- Chopped pistachios, optional

INSTRUCTIONS:
a) Pulse cannoli shells in a food processor until coarse crumbs form. Add sugar, cracker crumbs, and melted butter; pulse just until combined. Press onto the bottom and upsides of a greased 9-inch. pie plate. Refrigerate until firm, about 1 hour.

b) Beat the first 4 filling **INGREDIENTS:** until blended. Beat in ricotta cheese and extracts. Stir in chocolate chips. Spread into crust.

c) Refrigerate, covered, until set, about 4 hours. If desired, top with pistachios.

74. Pistachio and Sprinkles Cannoli

Makes: 16 servings

INGREDIENTS:
- 1½ cup Whole-milk ricotta cheese; well drained
- 3 tablespoons Sugar
- 1½ teaspoon Cinnamon
- 1 cup All-purpose flour
- 1 tablespoon Sugar
- 1 tablespoon Butter or lard
- 4 tablespoons To 5 Tbl sweet Marsala wine
- 1½ cup Milk chocolate; coarsely chopped
- ¼ cup Pistachio nuts; coarsely chopped or dry white wine
- 2 cups Vegetable oil
- Colored sprinkles
- Confectioners' sugar

a) In a bowl, combine all the filling **INGREDIENTS:** and mix well.

b) Refreigerate, covered, until ready to fill the cannoli shells.

c) To make the dough, place the flour in a bowl or food processor. Add the butter or lard and sugar and mix with a fork, or pulse, until the mixture resembles coarse meal.

d) Slowly add the ¼ cup of wine and shape the mixture into a ball; add a little more wine if the dough appears too dry.

e) It should be soft but not sticky. Knead the dough on a floured surface until smooth, about 10 minutes. Wrap the dough and refrigerate for 45 minutes.

f) Place the chilled dough on a floured work surface. Divide the dough in half. Work with 1 piece of dough at a time; keep the remaining dough refrigerated.

g) Roll the dough out to a very thin long rectangle about 14 inches long and 3 inches wide, either by hand or using a pasta machine set to the finest setting. Cut the dough into 3-inch squares.

h) Place a cannoli form diagnoally across 1 square. Roll the dough up around the form so the points meet in the center. Seal the points with a little water. Continue making cylinders until all the dough is used.

i) In an electric skillet, heat the vegetable oil to 375F. Fry the cannoli 3 or 4 at a time, turning them as they brown and blister, until golden brown on all sides. Drain them on brown paper. When they are cool enough to handle, carefully slide the cannoli off the forms.

j) To serve, use a long iced tea spoon or a pastry bag without a tip to fill the cannoli with the ricotta cheese mixture. Dip the ends into colored sprinkles, arrange them on a tray, and sprinkle confectioner's sugar over the tops. Serve at once.

75. Orange Curacao Cannoli

Makes: 12 Servings

INGREDIENTS:
- 1¾ cup Flour; approximately
- 1 tablespoon Sugar
- ¼ teaspoon Salt
- 1 teaspoon Cinnamon
- 3 tablespoons Wine vinegar
- 1 Egg
- 1 tablespoon Butter or margarine; at room temperature
- 1 pounds Ricotta cheese
- ½ cup Confectioner's sugar
- ¼ teaspoon Vanilla extract
- 2 tablespoons Finely minced candied orange peel; or citron
- 3 tablespoons Chocolate
- ½ teaspoon Cinnamon
- 2 tablespoons Orange Curacao; (optional)
- 1 Egg white; to brush
- ¼ cup Chopped pistachio; or other nuts to garnish; (optional)
- 1 tablespoon Confectioner's sugar; to sprinkle
- Oil; for deep frying

a) Use your electric mixer. In a mixing bowl measure 1 cup flour, sugar, salt and cinnamon.

b) Attach bowl and dough hook. Turn to medium-slow speed and blend for approximately 45 seconds. With the mixer running, add vinegar, water, egg and butter. Mix to blend for 2 to 3 minutes.

c) Add remaining flour, ¼ cup at a time, as needed to make a dough that clings to the hook.

d) Knead for 5 minutes. If dough clings to the sides of the bowl, add sprinkles of flour. Dough will be smooth and elastic.

e) Wrap the soft dough in foil or plastic and refrigerate to relax and chill for at least 1 hour.

f) Heat at least 2 inches of vegetable oil to 375 degrees.

g) Place dough on a floured work surface and roll extremely thin-- 1/16 inch or less! Don't rush.

h) When the dough pulls back, allow it to relax. If it softens and sticks, return it to the frig for 5 or 10 minutes.

i) Cut 4½ inch circles (size of a many small margarine tub lids!)

j) Roll the dough scraps out and continue until all dough is used. You should have 12 to 14 circles.

k) When the circles are cut, roll again just before placing on the cannoli tubes. This will give them an oval shape, about 5 inches by 4 ½ inches.

l) Place the dough so that its longest dimension is the length of the metal tube. Brush the tip of the dough with egg white to seal. Toll dough on the tube.

m) Deep frying. The length of time will depend of the thickness of the shells. A very thin shell will need about 2 minutes. A thicker shell could require up to 6 minutes. Fry two or three at a time.

n) Turn over once during frying. Fry until golden brown. Remove with tongs. Cool for a few minutes and then push the tubes free to use again. Cool shells completely before filling.

FILLING:

o) Cream ricotta cheese in a bowl with a spatula or wooden spoon or with an electric mixer until smooth, about 5 minutes.

p) Add confectioners' sugar, vanilla, candied fruit, chocolate, cinnamon and orange curacao. Continue beating another 4 or 5 minutes. Refrigerate until ready to fill shells.

q) Use a small spoon to stuff the filling into the shells. Dip the ends in chopped nuts. Sift confectioners' sugar over the shells and serve.

76. Cannoli alla siciliana

Makes: 12 servings

INGREDIENTS:
SHELLS:
- 2 cups All-purpose flour
- 2 tablespoons Shortening
- 1 teaspoon Sugar
- ¼ teaspoon Salt
- ¾ cup Wine, Marsala, Burgundy or Chablis
- Vegetable Oil

FILLING:
- 3 cups Ricotta
- ½ cup Confectioners sugar
- ¼ cup Cinnamon
- ½ Square unsweetened
- Chocolate grated OR
- ½ tablespoon Cocoa (both optional)
- ½ teaspoon Vanilla
- 3 tablespoons Citron peel, chopped
- 3 tablespoons Orange peel, candied,chopped
- 6 Glace cherries, cut up

a) To make cannoli shells it is necessary to have 3 or 4 metal tubes, preferably made from very light tin, about 7-inches long and 1⅛ inches in diameter. The edges should not be soldered.

b) SHELLS: Combine flour, shortening, sugar and salt, and wetting gradually with wine, knead together with fingers until rather hard dough or paste is formed. Form into ball, cover with cloth and let stand about 1 hour.

c) Cut dough in half and roll half of dough into a thin sheet about ¼ inch thick. Cut into 4 inch squares.

d) Place a metal tube diagonally across each square from one point to another, wrapping dough around tube by overlapping the two points and sealing overlapping points with a little egg white.

e) Meanwhile heat vegetable oil in large deep pan for deep frying. Drop one or two tubes at a time into hot oil.

f) Fry gently until dough is a golden brown color.

g) Remove from pan, let cool and gently remove shell from metal tube.

h) Set shells aside to cool. Repeat procedure until all shells are made.

i) FILLING: Mix ricotta thoroughly with sifted dry ingredients. Add vanilla and fruit peel. Mix and blend well. (A little grated pistachio may be added if desired). Chillin refrigerator before filling shells. Fill cold cannoli shells; smooth filling evenly at each end of shell.

j) Decorate each end with a piece of glace cherry and sprinkle shells with confectioners sugar. Refrigerate until ready to serve.

77. Cannoli cream pizza

Makes: 1 Servings

INGREDIENTS:
- Dessert Pizza Shells
- 1 cup Confectioners' sugar
- 6 cups Ricotta cheese, well drained
- 1¼ cup Candied fruit, fine chopped
- 2 teaspoons Vanilla extract
- 2 ounces Semisweet miniature chocolate chips
- Unsalted pistachios, coarsely chopped
- Unsweetened cocoa powder

In a food processor or mixing bowl, whip the confectioners' sugar with the ricotta cheese until smooth and creamy. Fold in the candied fruit, vanilla and chocolate chips. Chill, covered, for two to three hours before using.

Put a layer of the cannoli cream over the baked pizza shell. Sprinkle the chopped pistachios over the cheese. Dust lightly with cocoa powder if desired.

78. Cannoli with hazelnut cream

Makes: 6 servings

INGREDIENTS:
- 1 cup Hazelnuts; shelled
- 2 cups Heavy cream
- ½ cup Granulated sugar
- ½ teaspoon Vanilla
- ¼ cup Pistachio nuts, shelled natural coarsely chopped
- 6 Cannoli shells
- Confectioner's sugar

a) Preheat oven to 350 F.

b) Scatter hazelnuts on a baking sheet and toast 15 to 18 mins, or until nuts are lightly browned and skins are cracked.

c) Remove as much of brown skins as possible by rubbing nuts in a kitchen towel.

d) Crack nuts into coarse pieces by enclosing in a clean kitchen towel and hitting gently with a rolling pin.

e) In a medium bowl, whip cream with an electric mixer 2 to 3 mins, or until thick. Briefly beat in granulated sugar and vanilla.

f) Fold in hazelnuts and pistachios. Stuff cannoli shells with nut cream.

g) Serve topped with a light sifting of confectioners' sugar.

79. Chocolate pistachio cannolis

Makes: 12 Servings

INGREDIENTS:
- ½ pack (11.5-oz) Nestle Toll House milk chocolate morsels
- 1 carton (15-oz) Ricotta cheese
- 2 packs (3-oz) cream cheese; softened
- 2 tablespoons Sifted confectioners' sugar
- 2 tablespoons Chopped citron
- 1 teaspoon Vanilla extract
- 12 Prepared 5-inch cannoli shells
- ⅓ cup Finely chopped pistachio nuts

a) Melt over hot (not boiling) water, Nestle Toll House milk chocolate morsels; stir until smooth.

b) Remove from heat; cool to room temperature. In large bowl, beat ricotta cheese until smooth.

c) Add cream cheese, confectioners' sugar, citron and vanilla extract; beat well. Blend in melted morsels.

d) Spoon into cannoli shells.

e) Dip ends in nuts. Chill until ready to serve.

80. Low-fat cannoli with raspberry sauce

Makes: 6 Servings

INGREDIENTS:
- 2 Containers; (15 oz) nonfat ricotta cheese
- 12 Wonton; (4 in.) wrappers
- Butter-flavored cooking spray
- 1 teaspoon Cornstarch dissolved in 1 tsp water; (for paste)
- 6 tablespoons Sugar
- ½ teaspoon Vanilla extract
- ¼ teaspoon Almond extract
- 3 cups Fresh raspberries
- 2 tablespoons Confectioners' sugar; up to 4
- 2 teaspoons Lemon zest
- 1 tablespoon Chopped; lightly toasted pistachio nuts

a) Drain ricotta 6 to 8 hours

b) Preheat oven to 400 degrees F. Lightly spray 12 cannoli tubes with cooking spray. Starting at corners, wrap wontons around tubes. Glue with dab or cornstarch paste. Lightly spray outsides of cannoli. Place on a baking sheet and bake until golden brown and crisp, about 4 to 6 min. Allow to cool slightly, then slide pastry off tubes. Cool on a wire rack.

c) Filling: In a large bowl, whisk ricotta, sugar, and extracts. Set aside or transfer to a pastry bag fitted with a ½-in. star tip.

d) Sauce: Puree raspberries in a food processor. Strain puree through a sieve into a bowl. Whisk in confectioners' sugar and lemon zest. (Recipe can be prepared several hours in advance up to this stage.)

e) Using pastry bag or teaspoon, insert ¼ c mixture into each shell.

f) Sprinkle ends with chopped pistachios. To serve, ladle raspberry sauce onto dessert plates.

Place 2 cannoli on each plate atop raspberry sauce and serve immediately.

81. Wonton cannoli

Makes: 4 Servings

INGREDIENTS:
- 24 wonton skins
- Peanut oil for deep frying
- Coarsely ground unsalted pistachio nuts
- Additional confectioners' : sugar
- Mint sprigs

FILLING:
- 1 lb lowfat Ricotta cheese, beaten smooth
- ½ c sifted confectioners' sugar
- 1 ts pure vanilla extract
- ⅓ c shaved semisweet chocolate

a) Heat oil in deep fryer to 375. Work with 6 wonton skins at a time.

b) Keep remainder well wrapped in waxed paper and draped with lightly dampened towel. Place a wonton skin on work surface and set a cannoli tube diagonally across center of it. If you don't have a cannoli tube, form a tube with some aluminum foil. Bring sides of skin up over tube. Seal overlapping tips with a dab of water. Form wonton skins around remaining 5 tubes. Cook, 2 tubes at a time, seam side down in hot oil, for 30 seconds or just until golden. Remove with tongs and drain on paper toweling. While shells are still hot, gently push them off tubes with a small metal spatula and your fingers.

c) Repeat with remaining skins and be sure tubes cool completely before wrapping with skins.

Filling:

d) Combine ricotta, confectioners' sugar, Vanilla and chocolate.

e) Cover and chill 2 hours or overnight. To serve: spoon filling into cannoli shells. A pastry bag will be very helpful here, or cut a corner off of a sandwich bag and squeeze the mixture out of it. Dip each end of filling in pistachios. Arrange on serving plate. Sift additional sugar over each and garnish with mint sprigs.

82. Cannoli stuffed with fresh fruit Srikhand

Makes: 4 servings

INGREDIENTS:
- 1 cup All purpose flour
- 1 tbsp ghee
- 1 tsp cardamom powder
- Fresh Fruit Srikhand
- 500 gm curd
- 1 cup powdered sugar
- 1/2 cup fresh fruits chopped
- as needed Pistachios powder for garnish

INSTRUCTIONS:
Add ghee and cardamom to flour and knead dough with required water. Cover and rest it for 10 minutes.

Roll out puri out of dough and stick it on cannoli pipes.

Fry it in hot oil at medium flame until crisp and done.

Tie curd in cloth and hung until water is removed. Add sugar powder to hung curd and pass it through the srikhand cloth. Nice homemade unflavored srikhand is ready. Add chopped fresh fruits. Here you can add any flavor or dry fruits.

Fill up crispy cannoli with srikhand and cover it with pistachio powder.

Prepare all cannoli accordingly and enjoy this Italian dessert with Indian twist.

83. Cannoli Delight with Pistachios

Makes: 4 servings

INGREDIENTS:
- 1 cup maida / all purpose flour
- 1 tbsp homemade ghee
- 1/2 cup semolina
- 1/2 tsp cinnamon powder
- 2 tbsp powdered sugar
- 1 cup sugar
- 2 tbsp watermelon seeds
- 4-5 black peppercorns
- 1 tbsp basil/ tulsi seeds
- 1 tbsp fennel seeds
- 8-10 almonds
- 1 cup mawa/ khoya
- 2 tbsp chopped dates
- 1 cup dark chocolate compound
- 2-3 tbsp grated pistachio
- 2-3 tbsp castor sugar
- 1 tbsp jam
- as per requirement Water
- as per requirement Salt
- as per requirement Oil

INSTRUCTIONS:
a) For making the cannoli shells, mix 1 cup maida, 1/2 cup semolina, 1/2 tsp cinnamon powder, 2 tbsp powdered sugar, a pinch of salt, 1 tbsp homemade ghee and water to make a thick dough. Let it rest for about 25-30 minutes.

b) For the filling, roast 2 tbsp watermelon seeds, 1 tbsp basil/ tulsi seeds, 1 tbsp fennel seeds, 8-10 almonds, and 4-5 black peppercorns till they become crunchy. Then let it cool and blend it in a mixer along with 1 cup of sugar.

c) In the same pan add 1 cup of mawa/ khoya. Add 2 tbsp chopped dates. Mix well, remove all the lumps and let the mawa cook. Remove from the flame and let it cool.

d) Add the blended seeds mixture to the mawa-dates mixture along with 2 tbsp of milk and mix well. Filling is ready.

e) Cannoli can be made by using the cannoli rolls that are easily available in the market. Here I have used aluminium recyclable tin.

f) Cut all the 4 sides of the tin to use the base. Roll the base into a roll and seal both sides using stapler.

g) Take a pedha size ball from the shells mixture and roll it on a flat surface by using rolling pin. Cut into square shape by using a cutter. Prick the squares by using a fork to prevent them from getting bubbles while frying.

h) Roll the square around the aluminium tin roll and seal the edges by using wheat flour and water mixture.

i) Heat oil for deep frying. Put the shells in the oil for deep frying (along with the aluminium rolls). Fry on low to medium flame to prevent them from getting burnt.

j) Once deep fried while they are still warm, remove the aluminium tin roll from the cannoli shell.

k) Melt 1 cup dark chocolate compound in a microwave or by using double boiler method. Dip both the sides of cannoli shells in the melted chocolate compound.

l) While the chocolate is still wet sprinkle grated pistachio on the chocolate. Let it set completely.

m)   Fill the cannoli shells with the filling. Once filled, arrange the cannolis on serving plate, and sprinkle castor sugar by using a strainer. Apply a jam dot in the center of cannoli and serve.

84. Italian Cannoli bites with pistachios

INGREDIENTS:

FOR THE CANNOLI SHELL
- 2 Cups all purpose flour
- 2 1/2 tbsp castor sugar
- 1 tsp cocoa powder
- 1/2 tsp cinnamon
- 1 pinch nutmeg (optional)
- 1/2 tsp salt
- 1/4 cup butter, melted
- 6-8 Tbsp apple juice or grape juice
- 2 Tbsp white wine vinegar
- Vegetable oil cooking spray

CANNOLI FILLING
- 12 oz whole milk Ricotta cheese, strained
- 8 oz Mascarpone cheese
- 1/2 cup powdered sugar
- 1/3 cup mini semi-sweet chocolate chips
- powdered sugar, for dusting (optional)

TOPPINGS:
- Melted chocolate, chopped pistachios, sprinkles, toasted sweetened coconut

INSTRUCTIONS:

a) Preheat the oven to about 200 degrees C.

b) Add flour, granulated sugar, cocoa powder, cinnamon, nutmeg and salt to a food processor and pulse until blended. Pour in melted butter and pulse until well combined then pulse until blended. In a bowl combine juice and vinegar, with processor running slowly pour in juice mixture and pulse just until mixture begins to come together.

c) Divide dough into two pieces, shape into balls and transfer to a resealable bag. Chill in refrigerator 30 minutes - 1 hour.

d) Meanwhile prepare filling. In a mixing bowl, using a rubber or silicone spatula, blend together Ricotta and Mascarpone cheese while running and pressing mixture along bottom of bowl to remove any lumps. Fold in powdered sugar. Cover and chill 30 minutes.

e) Roll each chilled dough out on a lightly floured surface into a 14-inch circle, to about an 1/8-inch thickeness. Cut into circles using a 2 1/2-inch round biscuit cutter.

f) Transfer rounds to an ungreased mini muffin tin, pressing evenly into sides and bottom of muffin well. Spray tops evenly with vegetable oil spray.

g) Bake in preheated oven 11 - 13 minutes until lightly golden.

h) Remove from oven and transfer to a wire cooling rack to cool completely. Once cool dip tops in chocolate if desired then into coating if using (such as pistachios) and allow chocolate to set.

i) Remove cannoli filling from refrigerator, transfer to a piping bag fitted with a tip (or you can use a large resealable bag and cut the tip of the end). Pipe filling into cups and sprinkle with chocolate chips and dust with powdered sugar. For best results serve within 2 hours. Store in refrigerator.

85. Cannoli Cones

INGREDIENTS:
1 lb Ricotta cheese

10 Sugar cones

4 oz ounces dark chocolate, coarsely chopped and melted

3 tbsp finely chopped salted, roasted pistachios

1/2 cup confectioners' sugar

2 tsp Marsala wine

1/2 vanilla bean, split and scraped, pod reserved for another use

2 tbsp finely chopped candied orange peel

2 tbsp mini chocolate chips

INSTRUCTIONS:
Place ricotta in a fine sieve set over a bowl; cover with plastic wrap. Refrigerate until drained, at least 2 hours or overnight.

Break off a portion of the top of each cone to create a 1 1/2-inch-deep arc on 1 side. Holding each cone at an angle, dip about 1/4 inch of rim into melted chocolate, and immediately sprinkle with pistachios, reserving some for garnish. Transfer to a parchment-lined sheet, broken side up. Refrigerate

Mix together ricotta, sugar, wine, and vanilla seeds. Mix in orange peel and chocolate chips.

Transfer ricotta filling to a pastry bag fitted with a large open-star tip. Pipe filling into cones. Sprinkle with reserved pistachios. Serve immediately.

86. Cannoli Pistachio Cupcakes

INGREDIENTS:
2 cup cake flour
1 ¼ cup unbleached all-purpose flour
1 Tbsp. baking powder
1 tsp. cinnamon
½ tsp. salt
1 ½ cup sugar
1 cup unsalted butter, room temperature
4 large eggs
1 cup whole milk
1 tsp. vanilla extract
cannoli filling (recipe follows)
mascarpone buttercream (recipe follows)
chopped pistachios
cannoli shells (optional)

INSTRUCTIONS:
Preheat oven to 325°F. Line 16-18 muffin pans with paper liners; set aside. Whisk flours, baking powder, cinnamon, and salt in a bowl; set aside. Cream butter and sugar, mixing until just light and fluffy. Add eggs 1 at a time until combined, scraping down the bowl after each addition. Add flour mixture in three batches, alternating with two additions of milk and vanilla to batter until completely mixed scraping down the bowl as you mix. Scoop batter into baking cups filling about 2/3 full. Bake until a cake tester inserted in the center comes out clean, 17 to 20 minutes.

87. Cannoli Sandwich Cookie

INGREDIENTS:
- 1 c butter, softened
- 3/4 c sugar
- 1/4 c brown sugar, packed
- 1 large egg
- 1 tsp vanilla extract
- 2 1/4 c flour
- 1 1/2 tsp baking powder
- 1/2 tsp orange zest
- 1/4 tsp cinnamon
- 1/2 c finely chopped pistachios
- melted chocolate

CANNOLI FILLING:
- 3/4 c whole milk ricotta
- 8 oz. mascarpone cheese
- 1/3 c powdered sugar
- 3/4 tsp vanilla

INSTRUCTIONS:
a) Beat butter at medium speed until creamy. Gradually add sugar and brown sugar, beating well. Add egg and vanilla, beat till combined.

b) Combine flour, baking powder, zest, and cinnamon. Add to butter mixture. Beat at medium speed. Stir in pistachios.

c) Shape dough into 2 - 6 inch logs. Wrap with wax paper and freeze until firm. Slice frozen dough into 1/8 inch thick rounds. Place rounds on a parchment paper lined cookie sheet.

d) Bake at 350 degrees F for 10-12 minutes, or until lightly browned at edges. Cool 1 minute on pan. Cool completely on wire rack.

e) Fill with cannoli filling. Assemble sandwiches and drizzle with melted chocolate. Cool in refrigerator until chocolate has hardened.

f) CANNOLI FILLING

g) Mix **INGREDIENTS:** together. Fill a pastry bag or Ziploc bag with filling. Chill until ready to use. To fill sandwiches, pipe filling on the underside of one cookie. Top cookie with another.

88. No-Bake Chocolate Chip Cannoli Cheesecake

Makes: 8 servings

INGREDIENTS:
- 1 package (4 ounces) cannoli shells
- 1/2 cup sugar
- 1/2 cup graham cracker crumbs
- 1/3 cup butter, melted

FILLING:
- 2 packages (8 ounces each) cream cheese, softened
- 1 cup confectioners' sugar
- 1/2 teaspoon grated orange zest
- 1/4 teaspoon ground cinnamon
- 3/4 cup part-skim ricotta cheese
- 1 teaspoon vanilla extract
- 1/2 teaspoon rum extract
- 1/2 cup miniature semisweet chocolate chips
- Chopped pistachios, optional

INSTRUCTIONS:
a) Pulse cannoli shells in a food processor until coarse crumbs form. Add sugar, cracker crumbs and melted butter; pulse just until combined. Press onto bottom and up sides of a greased 9-in. pie plate. Refrigerate until firm, about 1 hour.

b) Beat the first 4 filling **INGREDIENTS:** until blended. Beat in ricotta cheese and extracts. Stir in chocolate chips. Spread into crust.

c) Refrigerate, covered, until set, about 4 hours. If desired, top with pistachios.

89. Lemon strawberry mousse cake

Makes: 1 servings

INGREDIENTS:
- 1 cup All-purpose flour 250 mL
- ⅓ cup Toasted hazlenuts or pistachio nuts; finely chopped
- 2 tablespoons Granulated sugar 25 mL
- ½ cup Unsalted butter; cut into small pieces 125 mL
- 1 Egg yolk 1
- 1 tablespoon Lemon juice 15 mL
- 2 ounces Homemade or commercial sponge cake 60 g
- 4 cups Fresh strawberries 1 L
- 1 Envelope unflavoured gelatin 1
- ¼ cup Cold water 50 mL
- 4 Egg yolks 4
- ¾ cup Granulated sugar; divided 175 mL
- ¾ cup Lemon juice 175 mL
- 1 tablespoon Finely grated lemon peel 15 mL
- 4 ounces Cream cheese 125 g
- 1¾ cup Whipping cream 425 mL
- Chopped toasted pistachio nuts
- Sifted icing sugar

Preheat oven to 375F/190C.

To make pastry, in large bowl, combine flour with nuts and granulated sugar. Cut in butter until it is in tiny bits.

Combine egg yolk with lemon juice. Sprinkle over flour mixture and gather dough together into a ball. Roll or press to fit bottom of 9 or 10 inch/23 or 25cm springform pan.

Bake for 20 to 25 minutes, or until lightly browned. Break sponge cake into small pieces and and sprinkle on top of pastry.

Reserve eight of the best strawberries for the top. Hull remaining berries.

Cut about twelve even sized berries in half and arrange around edge of pan with cut side of berries pressed against the edge. Arrange remaining berries to fit inside pan with tips pointing up.

To make the filling, sprinkle gelatin over cold water in a small saucepan.

Allow to soften for 5 minutes. Heat gently until dissolved.

In medium saucepan, beat 4 egg yolks with ½ cup/125 mL granulated sugar until light. Beat in lemon juice and peel. Cook, stirring constantly, until mixture thickens and just comes to the boil. Stir in dissolved gelatin.

Cool.

In large bowl, beat cream cheese with with remaining ¼ cup/50 mL granulated sugar. Beat in cool lemon cream.

In separate bowl, beat whipping cream until light. Fold into lemon cream.

Pour over berries. Shake pan gently so lemon mixture falls between berries and top is even. Refrigerate for 3 to 4 hours, or until set. Run knife around edge of pan and remove sides. Place cake on serving platter. (Remove springform bottom only if it comes away easily.) Arrange 1 inch/2½ cm strips of waxed paper on top of the cake, leaving spaces in between. Sprinkle spaces with pistachio nuts. Remove paper carefully. Leave hulls on reserved berries and cut in half. Arrange berries in rows along empty strips. Dust with icing sugar. Refrigerate until ready to serve.

90. Sweet Filo Cigars

Makes: ABOUT 12 CIGARS

INGREDIENTS:
1 cup / 80 g sliced almonds
½ cup / 60 g unsalted pistachios, plus extra, crushed, to garnish
5 tbsp water
½ cup / 80 g vanilla sugar
1 large free-range egg, separated, white beaten
1 tbsp grated lemon zest
filo pastry, cut into twelve 7½-inch / 18cm squares
peanut oil, for frying
½ cup / 180 g good-quality honey

In a food processor, bring the almond and pistachio together into a fine paste. Place the ground nuts in a frying pan and add 4 tablespoons of the water and the sugar. Cook over very low heat until the sugar has dissolved, about 4 minutes. Remove the pan from the heat and add the egg yolk and lemon zest, stirring them into the mixture.

Put 1 sheet of pastry on a clean surface. Spread about 1 tablespoon of the nut mixture in a thin strip along the edge closest to you, leaving ¾ inch / 2 cm clear on the left and right sides. Fold the two sides over the paste to hold it in at both ends and roll away from you to create a compact cigar. Tuck the top edge in and seal it with a little bit of the beaten egg white. Repeat with the pastry and filling.

Pour enough oil into a frying pan to come ¾ inch / 2 cm up the sides. Heat the oil over medium-high heat and fry the cigars for 10 seconds on each side, until golden.

Place the cigars on a plate lined with paper towels and allow to cool. Place the honey and the remaining 1 tablespoon water in a small saucepan and bring to a boil. When the honey and water are hot, lightly dip the cooled cigars in the syrup for a minute and stir gently until well coated. Remove and arrange on a serving plate. Sprinkle with the crushed pistachios and leave to cool.

91. Ghraybeh

Makes: ABOUT 45 COOKIES

INGREDIENTS:
¾ cup plus 2 tbsp / 200 g ghee or clarified butter, from the fridge so it is solid
⅔ cup / 70 g confectioners' sugar
3 cups / 370 g all-purpose flour, sifted
½ tsp salt
4 tsp orange blossom water
2½ tsp rose water
about 5 tbsp / 30 g unsalted pistachios

In a stand mixer fitted with the whip attachment, cream together the ghee and confectioners' sugar for 5 minutes, until fluffy, creamy, and pale. Replace the whip with the beater attachment, add the flour, salt, and orange blossom and rose waters, and mix for a good 3 to 4 minutes, until a uniform, smooth dough forms. Wrap the dough in plastic wrap and chill for 1 hour.

Preheat the oven to 350°F / 180°C. Pinch a piece of dough, weighing about ½ oz / 15 g, and roll it into a ball between your palms. Flatten it slightly and place on a baking sheet lined with parchment paper. Repeat with the rest of the dough, arranging the cookies on lined sheets and spacing them well apart. Press 1 pistachio into the center of each cookie.

Bake for 17 minutes, making sure the cookies don't take on any color but just cook through. Remove from the oven and leave to cool down completely. Store the cookies in an airtight container for up to 5 days.

92. Mutabbaq

Makes: 6

INGREDIENTS:
⅔ cup / 130 g unsalted butter, melted
14 sheets filo pastry, 12 by 15½ inches / 31 by 39 cm
2 cups / 500 g ricotta cheese
9 oz / 250 g soft goat's milk cheese
crushed unsalted pistachios, to garnish (optional)
SYRUP
6 tbsp / 90 ml water
rounded 1⅓ cups / 280 g superfine sugar
3 tbsp freshly squeezed lemon juice

Heat the oven to 450°F / 230°C. Brush a shallow-rimmed baking sheet about 11 by 14½ inches / 28 by 37 cm with some of the melted butter. Spread a filo sheet on top, tucking it into the corners and allowing the edges to hang over. Brush all over with butter, top with another sheet, and brush with butter again. Repeat the process until you have 7 sheets evenly stacked, each brushed with butter.

Place the ricotta and goat's milk cheese in a bowl and mash together with a fork, mixing well. Spread over the top filo sheet, leaving ¾ inch / 2 cm clear around the edge. Brush the surface of the cheese with butter and top with the remaining 7 sheets of filo, brushing each in turn with butter.

Use scissors to trim about ¾ inch / 2 cm off the edge but without reaching the cheese, so it stays well sealed within the pastry. Use your fingers to tuck the filo edges gently underneath the pastry to achieve a neat edge. Brush with more butter all over. Use a sharp knife to cut the surface into roughly 2¾-inch / 7cm squares, allowing the knife almost to reach the bottom but not quite. Bake for 25 to 27 minutes, until golden and crisp.

While the pastry is baking, prepare the syrup. Put the water and sugar in a small saucepan and mix well with a wooden spoon.

Place over medium heat, bring to a boil, add the lemon juice, and simmer gently for 2 minutes. Remove from the heat.

Slowly pour the syrup over the pastry the minute you take it out of the oven, making sure it soaks in evenly. Leave to cool for 10 minutes. Sprinkle with the crushed pistachios, if using, and cut into portions.

CONDIMENTS

93. <u>Avocado-Pistachio Pesto</u>

Makes: 1 CUP

INGREDIENTS:
- ½ tablespoon crushed garlic (about 1 medium-size clove)
- ½ teaspoon salt
- 1 cup shelled pistachio nuts
- 2 cups fresh basil, lightly packed
- 1 tablespoon lemon juice
- ½ cup chopped ripe avocado
- 1 tablespoon olive oil

Place the garlic and salt in a food processor. Process into small pieces. Add the pistachio nuts, and process into small pieces. Add the basil, lemon juice, avocado, and olive oil, and process until mixed well.

This pesto is best made fresh and consumed within a few hours of making. The parts exposed to air will begin to oxidize and turn brown in time, so you'll want to scoop away the top brown layer before using.

94. Goat cheese and pistachio spread

Makes: 1 Servings

INGREDIENTS:
- 2 packs (3 oz) goat cheese; softened
- ¼ cup Chopped pistachios
- 1 large Clove garlic; minced
- ½ teaspoon Salt
- 1 Stick; (1/2 cup) butter, softened
- ¼ cup Chopped fresh chives

a) In food processor, combine garlic and salt, let sit for 10-15 minutes.

b) Then add the goat cheese, butter and chives. Blend until smooth.

c) Stir in the pistachios, garnish with more chives.

d) Serve with crostini, crackers or a sliced baguette.

95. Pistachio Basil pesto

Makes: 1 Servings

INGREDIENTS:
- 1 cup Fresh basil
- 1 cup Shelled pistachio nuts
- 2 Cloves garlic; (up to 3)
- ½ cup Freshly grated Parmesan
- Olive oil

a) Put all the ingredients in the blender and mix - you might need up to ⅔ c. olive oil. The Parmesan will thicken it up. Serve over hot pasta.

b) PUMPKIN SEED PESTO: As above, but substitute pumpkin seeds for pistachios.

c) Add 5 grams of fresh spinach too, if you'd like.

DRINKS

96. Strawberry & Pistachio Smoothie

Servings: 4

INGREDIENTS:
3 cups frozen strawberries
1 cup shelled, roasted pistachios
1 cup unsweetened vanilla almond milk
1 1/2 tablespoons pure maple syrup
1 cup water

INSTRUCTIONS:
Place your pistachios in a bowl and completely cover with water. Soak for at least 3 hours or overnight if possible.

Drain the water and thoroughly rinse the pistachios. Put them in a blender.

Puree the remaining ingredients in the blender until smooth and creamy. Serve and enjoy!

97. Green Tea Gin

INGREDIENTS:
FOR THE GREEN TEA-INFUSED GIN
- 750ml bottle gin
- 1/4 cup green tea leaves

FOR THE SALTED PISTACHIO HONEY SYRUP
- 1/2 cup water
- 1/2 cup salted pistachios
- 1/2 cup honey

INSTRUCTIONS:
a) Combine all the ingredients and steep for 2 hours.
b) Strain out the tea leaves.

98. Incredible Hulk

INGREDIENTS:

- 2 scoops vanilla protein
- 1/2 Tablespoons sugar-free pistachio pudding mix
- Few drops peppermint extract
- 1 few drops green food coloring (optional)
- 8 oz. cold water or low-fat milk
- 3-5 ice cubes

INSTRUCTIONS:

a) Throw all ingredients into a blender for 30-60 seconds.

99. Berry Pistachio Smoothie

Makes: 1

INGREDIENTS:
- ¾ cup raspberries fresh or frozen
- ¼ cup strawberries fresh or frozen
- ½ orange
- 2 tablespoon pistachios
- 1 tablespoon honey
- ¼ cup milk or more as needed; any kind

INSTRUCTIONS
a) Place ingredients in a blender and pulse until smooth, about 1 minute.
b) Enjoy!

100. Pistachio Banana Smoothie With Avocado

Makes: 2

INGREDIENTS
- 2 frozen bananas
- 1 large handful (about 1 cup) frozen or fresh spinach
- 1 cup frozen cauliflower florets
- ¼ cup pistachios
- 2 cups water
- ¼ avocado
- 1 tablespoon chia seeds
- 2 servings vanilla protein powder

INSTRUCTIONS
a) Add all ingredients to a blender. Blend until smooth.
b) Keywords: Pistachio Banana Smoothie with Avocado

CONCLUSION

We hope this cookbook has inspired you to experiment with pistachios in your cooking and baking. With so many tasty recipes to choose from, there's no excuse not to try something new. Whether you're serving up a sweet treat or a savory dish, pistachios are sure to add a delicious and nutty flavor to your creations. Thank you for joining us on this culinary journey and we can't wait for you to enjoy all the delicious recipes in this book!.